HARPERCOLLINS
LEADERSHIP

AN IMPRINT OF HARPERCOLLINS

How to Grow Your Small Business

Also by Donald Miller

Building a StoryBrand

Marketing Made Simple

DONALD
MILLER

How to
Grow Your
Small
Business

*A 6-Step Plan to Help
Your Business Take Off*

HarperCollins
Leadership

An Imprint of HarperCollins

Published by HarperCollins Leadership, an imprint of HarperCollins Focus LLC.

Any internet addresses, phone numbers, or company or product information printed in this book are offered as a resource and are not intended in any way to be or to imply an endorsement by HarperCollins Leadership, nor does Harper-Collins Leadership vouch for the existence, content, or services of these sites, phone numbers, companies, or products beyond the life of this book.

Book design by Aubrey Khan, Neuwirth & Associates, Inc.
Interior graphics designed by Kyle Reid, Emily Pastina, and Caleb Faires.

ISBN 978-1-4002-2805-8 (eBook)
ISBN 978-1-4002-2695-5 (HC)

Library of Congress Cataloging-in-Publication Data
Library of Congress Cataloging-in-Publication application has been submitted.

Printed in the United States of America

23 24 25 26 27 LBC 5 4 3 2 1

Dedicated to small business owners everywhere

A full 25 percent of small businesses fail within the first year. Forty-five percent of small businesses fail within five years, and 65 percent fail within ten years. There are 33 million small businesses in America alone. Those businesses employ tens of millions more people than just the owners. Millions of people's dreams live or die based on the success of small business. In my view, small business is too big to fail. I wrote this book so yours won't.

Contents

1 | Leadership

2 | Marketing

Author's Note

If you need a small-business growth plan that will help you build a reliable, profitable operation, my hope is that you're holding it in your hand. These are the six frameworks and playbooks that have helped thousands of small-business owners build businesses that work. If you've ever felt as though you're managing chaos as you grow your small business, this book is for you.

Preface

Small-business owners live close to the bone. In small business, if you don't know how to make money, your business will die. Unlike large corporations, small-business owners do not have massive budgets that allow for mistakes or inefficiencies.

Still, the feeling that you are always "diving for dollars" can get exhausting. Sometimes small-business owners envy the relative security of larger businesses that perform like money-printing machines. Where do large corporations have small businesses beat? They have them beat in their systems and processes.

What small-business owners need, then, is a simple system of frameworks and playbooks that optimize their businesses for growth. Small-business owners need a way to create predictability and reliability in their day-to-day operations.

The Small Business Flight Plan at the back of this book will help you optimize your business for revenue and profit. The Flight Plan is an operations manual and a growth plan all in one. This book will walk you through the creation of your flight plan.

How to Grow Your Small Business is written in hindsight. These are the six frameworks and playbooks that helped me take my business from four employees to thirty while increasing our revenue fourfold in just six years. And our revenue wasn't the only thing that got better. Our profit percentage increased. The quality of our products improved. Our customer base expanded. And our team morale shot up. It turns out team members and customers alike appreciate working with a well-run organization.

Whether you operate your business by yourself or have one hundred employees or more, you will find this book useful.

Use *How to Grow Your Small Business* to create a growth plan that works. And don't forget to enjoy the journey. Growing a business is supposed to be fun, and when you install the frameworks and playbooks explained in this book, it will be. Enjoy the process.

How to Grow Your Small Business

Introduction

How Do We "Professionalize"
Our Small Business?

Years ago, a friend gave me the best business advice I've ever received. His advice was so concise it rang in my head like a bell for the next five years.

Bill had scaled his father's company into the billions and with that money bought and sold several more companies that succeeded as well. Bill knew what it took to run a business, and he knew what it took to grow one.

We were standing in my driveway after having talked for an hour or so. We'd talked about where my business was and where it could go. The future was limitless, yet I could tell there was something Bill didn't want to say. He'd been nothing but encouraging in the years I'd known him, but this time it was obvious he had some constructive criticism. I asked point blank what he was thinking.

He stood silently for a moment, measuring his thoughts. "Don," he finally said, lowering his head and taking off his glasses. "You need to professionalize your operation."

"That's your problem." He continued. "Until you profession-alize your operation, its potential is limited. The amount of money you make and your ability to have a positive impact on the world will be limited."

I'd never heard the term "professionalize your operation" before, but it rang true. My business revolved too much around me, and nobody (including me) knew exactly what they were supposed to do to make it grow. We had a vision, for sure, but we'd not built the reliable, predictable systems that would allow us to execute that vision.

What Bill saw, and what I now know, is that even though we were succeeding as a company, we were climbing straight into the s-curve that haunts most small businesses.

Can You Avoid the Dreaded "S-Curve"?

Every successful business has come face-to-face with the "s-curve." The s-curve follows a specific pattern—the business begins to grow, which is a great thing, and then a dreadful series of events that could make or break a company is put into action.

Imagine a business puttering quietly along—the first part of the s-curve. Then, their products begin to sell. Demand might even soar. It's magic. The business begins to grow. Customers like the product and they start telling their friends. Everything is great, right? All the business owner's problems seem to be behind them.

But, then, things take a turn.

The business owner is pulled out of their sweet spot, the sweet spot they were in when the company took off. They spend too much time trying to put out fires, and the business starts to decline because the owner is managing problems rather than continuing to create the magic that grew the company.

Then the problems get worse. They hire too many people because they anticipate growth. They order too many parts to make too many products. They extend their buyers' terms to attract more business. They allot too much money to marketing that doesn't work. They start seeing people around the office and aren't sure exactly what they do. Customers feel the effects in product delays, frantic messaging, and bad customer service. Sales begin to decline. They temporarily lower their prices to cover bills and, as a result, devalue their product. Overhead increases while revenue decreases. The owner takes out a line of credit and starts to dip into it. The owner starts losing sleep. Their family suffers. Soon, the business has to shut down and the owner has to get a job to pay down the line of credit.

All this despite the fact that they had a product people wanted.

How in the world can something so tragic happen as a result of buyer demand?

After that conversation with Bill, I knew I was headed into the s-curve. My sweet spot was creating content and dreaming up great products, but for the previous year I'd been attending meeting after meeting trying to put out fires.

I did not want what has happened to so many small businesses to happen to me. In a way, Bill's criticism was hopeful. It led me to discover there was something I could do to grow my small business the right way: If I "professionalized my operation," the s-curve could be avoided.

I took Bill's message to heart and accepted it as a challenge. And I'm glad I did. In professionalizing my business, my company was able to find its footing, and I was able to get back to doing what I do best: creating content. In fact, if I hadn't pro-fessionalized my operation I'd not have been able to write the book you're reading now.

In the seven years since that conversation, my small business has gone from about $3 million to nearly $20 million in revenue. During that time, we've maintained a significant profit margin. Even better: if I leave for a few weeks on vacation, the business performs as though I were still there.

How Can You Professionalize Your Small Business So That It Succeeds?

After talking to Bill, I looked around for ways to professionalize my small business, but the more I looked around, the more I realized nobody had created a playbook. There were plenty of books about leadership, marketing, and sales, but a simple, step-by-step plan to professionalize my small business so it ran reliably did not exist.

What follows is the playbook I needed back when Bill and I stood in my driveway. Yes, my team and I figured it out, but we did so by taking two steps forward and one step back—over and over again. I've included the steps forward in this book and have left the steps back in my "lessons learned" file. It turns out holding an optional yoga session to build community is not one of the foundational frameworks you need to professionalize your operation.

Perhaps "professionalizing your operation" is something you need to do too. Developing a series of systems and processes that allow your small business to run like a machine might be the step forward you've been looking for.

The six areas we addressed to professionalize our operation were:

1. **Leadership:** We cast a vision for our company that included **three economic priorities (chapter one)** and made sure every role in the company supported those priorities.
2. **Marketing:** We clarified our marketing message and **invited our customers into a story (chapter two)** in which their problems could be solved by purchasing our products.
3. **Sales:** We installed a sales framework that **made our customer the hero and learned to craft a million-dollar sales pitch that closed more sales and drove revenue (chapter three).**
4. **Products:** We **optimized our product offering (chapter four)** and focused on products that were in demand and profitable.
5. **Overhead and operations:** We kept our overhead lean by running a management and productivity playbook that **aligned the entire team by holding only five recurring meetings (chapter five).** We made sure every team member had clear objectives and was coached and encouraged.
6. **Cash flow:** We used five checking accounts to manage the money that came in and **protected cash flow (chapter six)** above everything else.

These six initiatives solved most of the problems that haunted my small business. When we fixed them, our business began to run like a predictable, reliable machine.

These days I spend the majority of my time creating content, meeting with clients, and being present with my family. I have about five meetings each week with various members of my team. In those meetings we share necessary information and make plans that cause the business to grow.

This is a different life than the one I was living before we implemented the six frameworks and playbooks. Before professionalizing my operation, I felt like my business was a machine and I was trapped inside it.

Of course, the transformation did not come easily. We spent hundreds of thousands of dollars on outside consultants and countless hours trying solutions that didn't work. But, in the end, it was these six steps that led to both peace of mind and growth.

You Need a Practical, Realistic Plan You Can Install within Six Months

Regardless of the products or services you sell, you will sell more if you build a machine that properly produces, promotes, sells, and distributes those products. This book is not only designed to transform your business, it's designed to transform *you* into a person who knows how to build a business that works. And once you know how to build a business, you can duplicate the process in as many businesses as you like.

Whether your business is business-to-consumer, business-to-business, digital, financial, industrial, content-focused, service-oriented, or anything else, every step you install from this playbook will make a positive difference in your bottom line.

If you do not take the six steps that will organize and grow your business, you will continue to struggle with the six reasons most small businesses fail. Those reasons are:

1. A failure to identify and prioritize economic objectives
2. A failure to market products with a clear message
3. A failure to sell in such a way that makes the customer the hero
4. The production of products that aren't in demand or profitable
5. Bloated overhead because of inefficient management and productivity
6. A mismanagement of cash and cash flow

None of these problems has to take you down. If you implement the six steps I lay out in this book, none of them will.

Consider this book your manual for professionalizing your operation. These six steps can be installed in the order presented in this book, or in the order that will address your most pressing problems. If you want, you can install each of these steps in six months, or you may decide to take a year or longer. With each step you address, you will see results in your bottom line. You will find that Step One alone—rewriting your Mission Statement to include three economic priorities—will help you find the focus you need to grow revenue and improve morale. Step Two will cause even more growth, and so on.

You do not need to implement all six frameworks for your business to grow, but the more you implement, the stronger your business will become and the less you will feel trapped inside the machine you built.

With that, let's look at a visual metaphor that will help you make sense of the six steps and also help you understand how a small business really works.

Build Your Business Like an Airplane or It Will Crash

In order to understand how to perfect our small business, we need a standard we can compare our business to so we can see which parts of our own business are engineered well and which parts need work.

You've likely met a person (or two) who is exceptional at business. You may have even thought these people have a gift. It's true that some people come off as business savants because of their ability to know what's wrong with a business after asking just a few questions. The truth is, though, they aren't savants. What they have is a standard to which they are comparing the business in question. This standard is allowing them to perform a fast comparison that reveals weaknesses.

This chapter will reveal that standard. Once you understand it, you will see your business (and everybody else's) clearly. I will then spend the rest of the book revealing how to fix each of the six critical parts of your businesses so it performs as close to the standard as possible.

The Airplane Is Our Standard

Back when my business was earning less than $250,000 in revenue per year, I had a model airplane on my bookshelf. One day, I was looking at the airplane and realized the way an airplane is engineered is similar to the way a business should be engineered. Like an airplane, a business has parts, and those parts connect to the whole to make it fly.

When it's built correctly, an airplane is a safe, reliable, and useful machine that will successfully do its job of taking precious people and cargo to a set destination. When it is not built to the correct specifications, however, it becomes a dangerous machine that could produce catastrophic results.

The primary goal in engineering an airplane is to get it to a specific destination without crashing. In order to stay in the air, it has to move forward, fast, so it must have a source of propulsion. In order to get lift, it needs to have wings that are strong and light. In order to carry people and cargo, it has to have a body that is as lean as possible so it doesn't add too much weight. Finally, the airplane must have enough fuel to reach its destination without running out and crashing.

A good commercial airplane has many parts, but six of them are absolutely crucial if it's going to fly safely.

The Six Parts of Your Small Business

I picked up the airplane and turned it around in my hands. There are six critical parts to a business, just like there are six critical parts to an airplane.

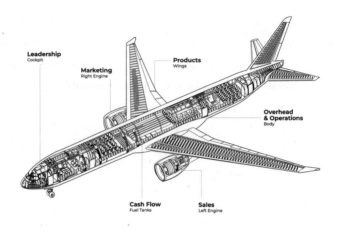

1. The cockpit of the airplane represents the leadership. Essentially, the leadership is in charge of getting the airplane to its destination. The pilot or pilots have to know where the plane is going and reverse engineer its safe arrival.

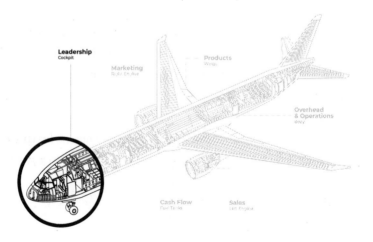

To grow a business, you'll need to know how to unite a team around a clear economic mission.

2. The right engine represents the marketing effort, which directly contributes to the airplane's thrust. When the marketing engine runs efficiently, the business sells more product and moves the business forward. This movement, in turn, contributes to lift.

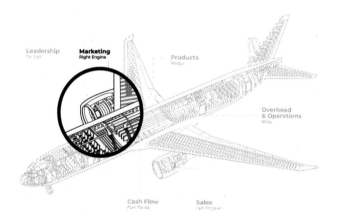

To grow a business, you will need to clarify your marketing message, so it produces a considerable amount of thrust.

3. The left engine represents sales, which increases the thrust of an airplane even more. Even if you don't have a sales team, you are likely involved in countless sales conversations. Unfortunately, most of us hate to sell. Nevertheless, when we learn to craft a million dollar sales pitch and invite customers into a story in which our products or services solve their problems, sales go up and the thrust that moves the plane forward increases.

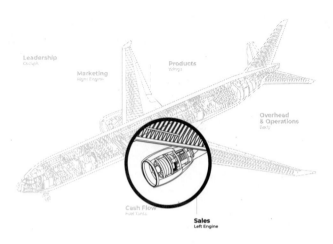

To grow a business, you will need to sell by making the customer the hero. Most people talk too much about themselves when they sell. Stop. Mastering sales conversations that invite customers into a story will increase the thrust of the airplane even more.

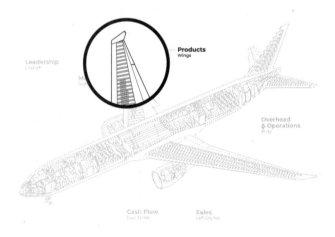

4. The wings of the airplane represent the products or services you sell. If the products or services you sell are in demand and profitable, they will give the business lift, and support the weight of the airplane. Thrust is provided through marketing and sales efforts, but the wings (profitable and in-demand products) make the airplane fly.

To grow a business, you need to know how to optimize your product offering so the airplane gets maximum lift.

5. The body of the airplane represents overhead and operations. If your overhead gets out of hand, the belly of the plane will grow too big, and the plane will crash. Your largest expense is almost always your payroll. Whether you are only paying yourself or a small staff, payroll will crash a business unless you and your team are running a management and productivity playbook.

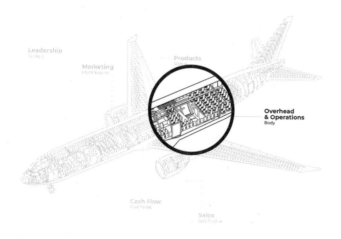

To grow a business, you'll need to run a management and productivity playbook that ensures every team member is contributing to the overall economic priorities of the business itself.

6. The fuel tanks represent cash flow. With fuel, energy is transferred to all the moving parts of the airplane. Without fuel, the plane crashes no matter how well it is designed. The same is true of cash for a small business. Cash must be managed so that there is enough money to operate, plus plenty of extra in case the plane has to circle the airport a few times to prepare for an emergency landing.

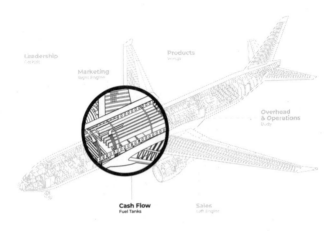

To grow a small business, you'll need a method for managing money that is simple and easy to use.

The Airplane Creates a Decision-Making Filter That Gives You Peace of Mind

The simple metaphor of the airplane created a powerful decision-making filter that allowed me to grow my business intuitively. For instance, whenever we hired a new team member, I'd ask myself how we would offset their salary. Would this investment make the wings larger (helping create a new product or revenue stream) or increase thrust (increasing sales) or enlarge the body of the airplane (increasing overhead and making it heavier, contributing to a crash)?

Keeping this metaphor in mind has allowed me to make smarter decisions, which, it turns out, is the key to growing a business. Growing a small business is all about making one smart decision after another and knowing how to recover when things don't work out the way you expected. Using the standard of the airplane, I was able to assess where my troubles were coming from and which of the six critical parts needed work in order to keep it flying.

In the years since I realized growing a business was a lot like building an airplane, I've taught this metaphor to thousands of other small-business owners. The results have been impressive. In fact, many small business owners just like you have doubled their revenue since implementing the frameworks. If you want your business to grow, all you need to do is work on the six parts of the airplane and connect them together so that it flies far and fast.

The steps included in this book will help you get your business off the ground and grow it to fifty or more employees or multiple millions in revenue. Once your business is off the ground, more frameworks and playbooks may be necessary to address more departments. Human resources comes into play the more team members you have, for example. Still, if you're just getting started or attempting to grow your small business into the hundreds of thousands or multiple millions, these are the areas you need to address first.

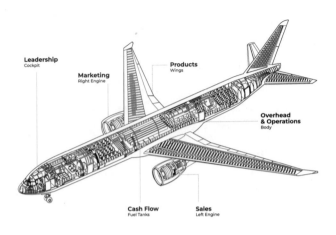

Obey the Rule of Proportion as You Grow and Your Business Won't Crash

In order to grow your business safely, you'll want to grow its parts in proportion to each other.

When your business is really small, it's just you in a cockpit with a single engine out front. You're humming along through the clouds and life is great. That engine is likely a marketing engine, perhaps a simple sales funnel or some Facebook ads or, if you're lucky, word of mouth. Your wings are likely small, but they're enough to lift you off the ground. You've got a product you're selling at the farmers market or on Etsy or perhaps a simple retail shop. Maybe you're doing some consulting or offering financial services or selling real estate or a network marketing product. Regardless, you have a product or service people are buying and your single-propeller marketing engine is enough to move a few units and put cash in your pocket. Your fuel tanks are small, but because the plane is small, you've got plenty of fuel to circle the airport a few times in case there is an emergency.

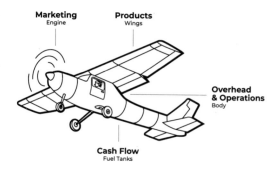

As your business grows, you are likely going to need help. Your first hire might be somebody to free up more of your time, so you hire a personal assistant. That hire contributes significantly to the overhead (makes the body of the airplane larger) and doesn't directly contribute to the size of the wings or increase thrust to the engines. It's a good thing to worry a little bit because the cost of the hire might put the safety of the plane at risk. However, when you consider the amount of time an assistant would allow you to contribute to the size of the wings or the thrust of the engine (perhaps as lead salesperson), you can more than justify the hire. The plane just got a little larger, but that doesn't matter because the wings and engine(s) got larger too.

Congratulations. You just started growing your business. Let's keep going.

Now that your overhead is a bit larger and your engine is humming a little louder, you're going to increase the size of your fuel tanks. You'll want six months of overhead sitting in a rainy-day account in case of an emergency. After saving six months of operating expenses, the airplane feels stable, so you start planning your next move.

Next, perhaps, you realize the marketing dollars you're spending would be better spent in house, so you hire a full-time marketing person. This position isn't cheap, but you can justify it because the new team member adds a second engine. Now there are three of you in the airplane: you, a personal assistant, and a marketing director. The plane's a little larger, but it's flying well.

After a year or so, you realize there are all sorts of special accounts interested in your products. If you had a salesperson, you could reach out to those accounts, so you hire a sales rep to create even more thrust. You pay them a small base salary and a healthy commission, so their position does not bloat the overhead. Commissions, after all, scale with success, which means the body of the airplane (overhead) only gets bigger when the actual thrust of the airplane increases.

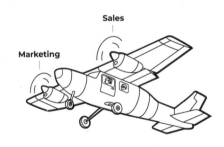

From here, you continue to alternate between hiring product creators, production team members, and marketing, sales, and administrative help. Since you hire team members proportionally and always keep an eye on overhead, your business grows with a limited amount of risk.

Not only this, but the business keeps growing from there. When you take the six steps, the steps themselves lead to growth while simultaneously helping you manage that growth.

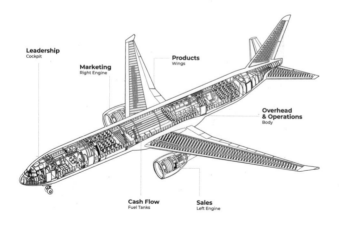

Unfortunately, the moves I described above are mismanaged by most small-business owners. Sometimes, the business owner hires before the right and left engines can support the added weight. Other times, the business owner waits too long to hire, resulting in unhappy customers and lost potential.

The reason most small businesses fail is not because people don't want the products they sell, it's because they didn't have a simple plan that made growing their small business intuitive. When we don't have the visual metaphor of the airplane in mind, we are still building an airplane; we are just building it wrong. If you build an airplane the wrong way, it won't fly. Or, worse, it will fly for a little while and then crash.

If you or someone you know has ever run a business that has failed, you can easily assess the postmortem using the analogy of the airplane. Remember, businesses usually fail for one of six reasons. Either the team failed to unify around economic objectives, the marketing message was not clear, the sales conversations didn't optimize sales results, the products weren't profitable or in demand, the overhead was bloated, or the business ran out of money.

You can easily avoid these six fatal flaws of small businesses. If you master the six steps that build your business like an airplane, your business will fly.

Beware of Looking Successful Without Being Successful

Sadly, many businesses, especially start-ups funded by outside sources like venture capital or private equity, can easily *look* successful without *being* successful. Beware. The leader of a start-up that is fully funded must still obey the rules of the airplane; otherwise, they will lose all their investors' money.

Too many start-up leaders check their bank accounts, see millions of dollars, and start to spend the money without wisdom. They usually start by paying a firm to create a brand identity. Because a lot of branding firms are more interested in making you look good than making you money, the start-up leader ends up with a great looking brand that confuses rather than attracts customers. They double down on their investment by putting their pretty logo all over a bunch of unnecessary swag that, again, makes them look good but doesn't sell products. Not only this, they get excited about their incredible funding and so they lease office space in an expensive part of town. They put their logo on the wall and invite friends over for happy-hour cocktails in which a ping-pong tournament breaks out and they all have more fun than they've had since college.

These kinds of decisions amount to an airplane with a massive body, tiny wings, weak engines, and a cockpit that more closely resembles a first-class cabin flowing with alcohol than a small room where serious pilots can study the numbers and fly the airplane.

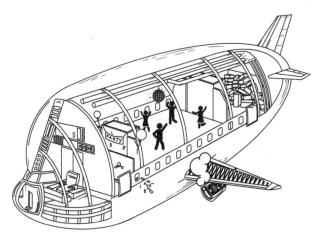

If you have started a small business and don't have the luxury of deep pockets backing you up, you may actually be at an advantage. Why? Because you are more in touch with the rules of physics that determine the success or failure of your business. Venture capital and private equity are amazing tools but if leadership is not careful they can cause serious disorientation when flying the plane.

To Build Your Business, Create a Small-Business Flight Plan

If you engineer an airplane without paying attention to the laws of physics, people are going to get hurt.

To engineer and build an airplane correctly, the companies that build large commercial and government airplanes use careful checklists. Later, when pilots fly the airplane, they continue to use checklists, as do the maintenance crews on the ground. For this reason, air travel is one of the safest forms of transportation.

What has been missing since the beginning of small business are checklists, frameworks, and playbooks you can trust to grow a business.

Many business leaders fail to professionalize their operations because doing so feels cumbersome and exhausting. Some business owners have told me that installing an overall business playbook takes more work than serving their customers. This makes them frustrated because they didn't sign up to build a business, they signed up to make or represent a product they love and sell those products to customers they care about. The business, in fact, seems to be the thing that gets in the way.

This shouldn't be the case.

The six steps that help you build your business like an airplane are easy to understand and simple to implement.

Use this book as a manual of flight checks to make sure your business is engineered the best possible way for maximum revenue, profit, and customer satisfaction.

Each of the steps in this book works like a mini book in itself. Implement the steps you need at the pace you believe you need to take them. You can keep coming back to *How to Grow Your Small Business* for months or even years. In fact, you can hand this book to your leadership team, review the Small Business Flight Plan together, and transform your business as a group.

The point is this: if you're spending too much time putting out fires and not enough time selling products and interacting with customers, you likely need to professionalize your operation.

To get the most from this book:

1. Review the flight plan in the back pages. Your flight plan includes all the templates you need to implement the six steps.
2. Read about each step and take them slowly. Each step will help you organize your small business and also generate growth.
3. Continue using the six steps associated with the flight plan to operate your business safely and profitably.

Taking off into the clouds can be exhilarating if you know what you're doing. Let's take the first step.

1

Leadership

STEP ONE:
The Cockpit

Become a Business on a Mission

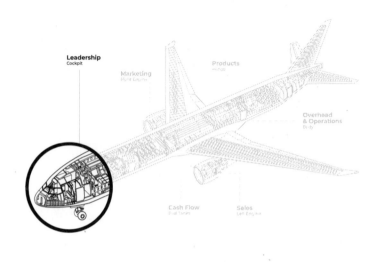

• • •

The primary job of the leader and the leadership team is to clearly define a destination and then reverse engineer a plan to get there. The second job of a leader or leadership team is to keep reminding team members about the destination and constantly make corrections to ensure a successful arrival.

When it comes to flying an airplane, much of what's needed for a successful flight hinges on the flight plan. Without a clearly defined destination, the pilot and crew cannot execute the tasks required to achieve their objective.

On commercial flights, pilots know exactly where the plane is supposed to be every minute of the flight. The predetermined coordinates may change a bit in the air, but it's the specific flight path that provides a filter for all decision-making during the flight.

The same should be true when it comes to leading a small business.

Most small businesses have goals, but those goals aren't spelled out clearly enough to help each team member understand the mission and their role within that mission. The problem is that the mission is too elusive and the rest of their Guiding Principles are forgettable. If our goal is to "Earn trust by satisfying customers," we are inviting team members into an elusive story that they cannot translate into action. However, if our goal is to "triple the number of coaching clients in the next twenty-four months," and their Critical Actions are to ask every customer if they know about the coaching program, the team better understands what to do. Why? Because the mission has been made specific and their Critical Actions are defined.

I'll explain more about how the three components of your Guiding Principles will inspire action in a moment. Sadly, an elusive mission is common with most small businesses. Many team members (and owners, for that matter) in the small-business environment aren't sure what they're supposed to be doing or, for that matter, where the business itself is trying to go.

Whether you're a solo-preneur or run a small business, the Mission Statement and Guiding Principle framework I'll share with you in Step One will clarify your company's objectives so you can become a business on a mission.

By completing Step One, *Become a Business on a Mission,* you will be creating a Guiding Principles package that includes three elements:

1. A Mission Statement that includes three economic priorities
2. Key Characteristics necessary for every team member

3. Critical Actions you can take every day that will unify
    your team and define your culture

When you are done with Step One, your Mission Statement and Guiding Principles will fit on a single sheet of paper you can review at important meetings. You will find that sheet of paper in your Small Business Flight Plan and can access a digital, fillable version at SmallBusinessFlightPlan.com. Once you know where you want your business to go, engineering its successful arrival will become more intuitive.

If you are going through this process alone, give yourself several days to finish Step One. Each element of your Guiding Principles package will require a bit of thought, so take your time. If you're creating your Guiding Principles as a team, give yourselves eight to ten hours to complete the assignments. You can do this by scheduling several two-hour meetings or giving an entire day to the process. In fact, many teams schedule an offsite event or retreat to complete their Guiding Principles.

This chapter will introduce you to the three parts of your *Business on a Mission* Guiding Principles package and walk you through the process step-by-step.

The Mission Statement and Guiding Principles Worksheet you will use to execute Step One looks like this:

Business on a Mission Guiding Principles Worksheet

MISSION STATEMENT

KEY CHARACTERISTICS

① ② ③

CRITICAL ACTIONS

① ② ③

Business Made Simple

Access a digital, fillable version at SmallBusinessFlightPlan.com

Use the rest of this chapter to understand the three parts of the Business on a Mission Guiding Principles Worksheet. Once you've filled out this worksheet in your Small Business Flight Plan at the back of this book, your business will be aligned around three economic priorities, you will know what sort of people you should have with you on the plane, and you will establish three Critical Actions that further ensure your success.

Business on a Mission, Part One: Your Mission Statement

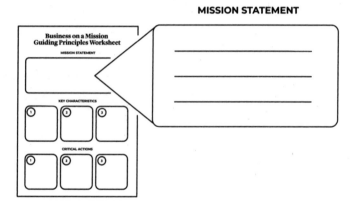

There are three reasons most Mission Statements fail:

1. They do not include specific economic objectives.
2. They do not include a deadline.
3. They do not answer the question "why?"

When you include these three elements in your Mission Statement, you effectively invite yourself and your team into an important story.

Why invite yourself and your team into a story? Every human being wants to play an important role in an important story. When you use our formula for an effective Mission Statement, you give your team more than just a mission—you give them a part to play in a story that is bigger than themselves. This, in turn, is going to improve morale, productivity, recruitment, and retainment. Everybody wants to work for a business on a mission.

Let's Face It, Most Mission Statements Are Forgettable and So They Are Forgotten

The sort of Mission Statements that get created by most businesses are anything but helpful.

Untold numbers of corporate Mission Statements read something like this: *We exist to increase stakeholder value by serving customers with integrity and excellence whereas by which we blah blah blah*, and so on.

A Mission Statement like this is missing one critical element: A mission.

Your company will live or die based on how clearly you articulate an engaging mission.

If you were assigning a mission to soldiers, wouldn't you feel the need to be clear? Saying "at some point, we are going to serve the common good by ridding the social landscape of dangerous insurgents so everyone can be free" is not clear enough to inspire the specific actions necessary to achieve an objective. However, saying "our mission is to clear and secure the dictator's compound from four sides and also from the air in order to save the hostages and take control of the area" is specific enough to inspire the right team to create the right plan and execute a series of actions to achieve the stated objective.

Equally, the director of a symphony will do no good to direct her orchestra to "play with excellence." The performance will be nonsense unless she directs her players to play Holst's *The Planets*, specifically, with excellence.

A Mission Statement that is specific inspires action; a Mission Statement that is vague causes confusion.

What if a confusing mission is holding your team back? Once each year you stand on a podium, lift your arms, and say something elusive like "do excellence," after which each and every member of your team starts playing different songs with excellence.

To Inspire Your Team, Open a Story Loop

If we want our teams to unite around a mission, we have to open a story loop in their minds that can only be closed if we accomplish that mission. Another problem with vague Mission Statements is that they fail to open a story loop. When you tell a story, the listener pays close attention to find out if, in fact, the hero will disarm the bomb or the man will marry the woman. Until the story is resolved, they feel (and enjoy) a slight uneasiness that causes them to pay attention until their sense of peace is restored. This discomfort is a mild form of cognitive dissonance.

A story, then, works like a puzzle. The mind sees disarray and wants to put things together in the right order, and when it does, we experience a sense of relief.

The desire to close a story loop is called narrative traction. Narrative traction is the point at which we get interested in a story. Here's why this matters for our businesses: When our

Mission Statement creates narrative traction, team alignment and productivity increase because we and our team get to work to close the story loop.

When a general tells their troops that they are going to secure the dictator's compound from all four sides as well as from the air, the imaginations in the ranks get to work, reverse engineering a plan that will allow them to secure the compound and close the story loop in their minds, relieving them of cognitive dissonance. When we are vague, though, a "plan" is never actualized because our team can't imagine how the story we are suggesting might end. This is why statements such as "we exist to serve customers with care and excellence" fail to inspire action. A statement like that is the equivalent of giving soldiers the mission to "be good and fight for good." Be good how? Fight who? To what end?

Be Specific

If you were to write a movie script that opens the story loop of a gentleman looking for something vague such as "excellence in all his doings," the audience will have trouble knowing what that means and a story loop will fail to open. However, if the hero of your story wants to "break the world record for the 100-yard dash," a story loop in the mind of the audience is opened and the story achieves narrative traction. Will our hero break the record? Let's stay engaged until we find out.

What would change if you created a Mission Statement that opened a clear enough story loop that you and your team felt a collective narrative traction that drove action?

When you install Step One, *Become a Business on a Mission,* you are going to do exactly that.

What we need to create a Mission Statement that drives narrative traction are **three economic objectives**, a **deadline**, and a **clear reason the mission is important**.

The *Business on a Mission* formula includes the coordinates for a very specific destination, a deadline, and a reason "why."

The Three Components of a Remarkably Effective Mission Statement

The first thing we will need to build a Mission Statement that actually works is to identify key sales metrics that will ensure your business succeeds.

Your mission statement should include three economic objectives. If everybody can understand exactly where the business is going, and that destination can be measured against a quantifiable metric, you've stated the mission clearly. When I say "measured against a quantifiable metric," I mean the objectives are best understood if they are expressed numerically.

If people feel confused after they read your Mission Statement or, worse, if team members have all sorts of questions (they won't actually ask for fear of looking stupid), your Mission Statement isn't clear and won't invite your team to move forward.

By stating numeric objectives such as "we will double our rate of customer retention" or "we will increase our revenue by 35 percent and increase our profit margin by 12 percent" or, better, "we will sell X number of Y products," we define a metric by which we know whether we did or did not accomplish our mission. This kind of measurable specificity is necessary to open a story loop that people must take action to close.

I'll explain more about what your three economic priorities should be soon; for now, let's look at the second element necessary to create narrative traction.

Second, it should include a deadline. When you give somebody an important assignment, you must also give them a deadline. You'd never hire a contractor to build a house without agreeing on a budget and a timeline, right? The assignment is too important. Isn't the mission of your business an important assignment? Of course it is.

Perhaps one of the reasons most Mission Statements don't include a deadline is because leaders believe a Mission Statement should last forever. That's one of the worst ideas when it comes to creating a Mission Statement. Can you imagine a sports team stating the mission to win the championship at some point in the next, say, one thousand years? That's a worthless mission because the mission doesn't have an actual deadline that creates a sense of urgency.

You can edit your Mission Statement every few years (and you should) because missions are meant to end. No mission that is open ended is going to inspire action.

A second reason people don't include a deadline in their mission is because they don't want to deal with the discomfort of having to achieve (or not achieve) their mission. The more elusive your Mission Statement is, the harder it will be to know if you've failed to achieve it.

Obviously, such a Mission Statement defeats the purpose. A good Mission Statement sets realistic goals and realistic deadlines rather than elusive goals and open-ended timelines you can hide behind.

The third thing your Mission Statement should include is a "reason" why the mission is important. Your mission needs a "why" or a "because" in order to invite you and your team's full heart into the mission itself.

People are not motivated by money alone, nor by winning and success. In fact, sometimes numeric and financial goals (while easy to measure) make people uncomfortable. You must make sure the story of achieving your mission is larger than the economic factors that allow your team to measure their progress.

Human beings are complex creatures. We want to do important work. We want to know our lives are making a difference. While it might be true that we could all make more money doing selfish things, almost everybody reading this book wants to build a business that serves customers and makes personal sacrifices to do so.

So how do we include a "because" in our Mission Statement? We make sure to mention what happens in the overall story of our customer when they encounter our products and services.

For instance, if you own a real estate office and want to sell one hundred homes this year, your Mission Statement might end with the phrase: ". . . because every person deserves to walk into a home they love."

This statement then serves as the reason your work is important. A real estate agent gets up every day because it brightens the lives of their clients when they find a home they love. Helping people find a home is important work. When the real estate agent includes the "why" in their Mission Statement, this inspires them and their office to do more great work and to do it well.

If you own a dental practice, you might say something like "because when people love their smile, they love themselves and their lives all the more."

Including a "because" at the end of your Mission Statement will help everybody involved understand why the mission is important.

The Three Elements That Create a Storyline

One of the biggest problems all businesses face is the challenge of engagement. How do we get our talent to fully engage in the work? And how do we attract and retain top talent?

Again, the best way to engage yourself and your workforce is to create narrative traction around your mission. Narrative traction happens when your Mission Statement posits such an engaging question that you can't wait to find out what happens. Will we surpass our competitor? Will we launch the new revenue stream? Will we double our sales of product X?

Your new Mission Statement defines that story and invites everybody to participate.

A Mission Statement Formula That Works

The best formula for a Mission Statement that includes all three elements necessary to create narrative traction goes like this:

We will accomplish **X** by **Y** because of **Z**.

When you use this formula to create your Mission Statement, you effectively enter economic coordinates for your business, you include a realistic deadline that increases a sense of urgency, and you define a reason the work is important. These three elements will also effectively invite you and your team into a story that will inspire action.

Now that we have a formula for creating a Mission Statement that works, let's create one for you, step-by-step.

Mission Statement Part One: Define Three Financial Priorities

Once we break away from all the fluffy language we love to use in Mission Statements and generate specific coordinates that can be used to make decisions, everybody on board the plane will know where we are going and can reverse engineer their job to make sure it supports those objectives.

But what kind of objectives should we prioritize?

In order to build a business that is dependable, the objectives we prioritize must be economic. If the business does not create profitable revenue, the business will stall and crash. If the business crashes, the mission will not be accomplished, customers' problems will not be solved, and the entire team will lose their jobs.

This catastrophe must be avoided.

Very few Mission Statements include economic objectives. I believe this is a mistake. The business exists to generate profit while creating value for customers. This should not be a hidden agenda.

Often, I meet team members within small businesses who believe that if you take care of customers, the money will take care of itself. Sadly, this is not true. Both the customers' needs and your bottom line must be watched at all times. The laws of commerce, just like the laws of physics, don't change. If a flight crew is extremely good to their customers but the plane runs out of gas, the story ends in tragedy all the same.

You don't have to live for the dollar, but you do need dollars to stay alive. Establishing financial priorities in our Mission Statement sets clear goals for the safe flight of our airplane.

Always remember you and your team are dependent on the success of this business. It must not crash.

Keep your business grounded in economic realities at all times. Not every team member wants to be in business to make money. Some team members would rather give products away and only be paid in gratitude. Unfortunately, that's a great way to crash a plane. These employees see the world this way because the business they work for does not belong to them. It's not their plane, it's your plane; and if they crash your plane, they can go work on somebody else's plane and crash that one too. Ironically, team members who are "not motivated by money" still expect a paycheck.

Let's make sure the "we don't care about money" mentality doesn't take over our small business. The truth is that caring about customers and caring about the bottom line are not mutually exclusive. Again, keep your business grounded in economic realities at all times.

You and Your Team Should Talk Openly about the Economic Priorities

The main reason to include three economic priorities in your Mission Statement is to normalize conversations around finances. If you and your team normalize conversations about money, you and your entire team will make more money. I promise.

In conversations with your leadership, you should consistently ask and answer questions like these:

- How much money are we making?
- How profitable is the business we are bringing in?

- What was our financial goal this month or this quarter?
- Did we reach that goal? Why or why not?
- How can the company improve? Should we change the economic priorities in our Mission Statement?
- How are the economic objectives not listed in our Mission Statement doing?

Why Should You Only Include Three Economic Priorities?

Your small business may have several economic objectives. You may want to sell a specific number of units, maintain a certain profit margin, or increase sales by X. In fact, you should have dozens of economic objectives. The reason we limit our Mission Statement to include only three economic objectives, though, is because the human brain has trouble prioritizing more than three objectives at a time. The adage is true: if you prioritize everything, you prioritize nothing.

Regardless, for most businesses, there are typically as few as three economic factors that will likely determine their success. There may be more, and you will certainly tend to those, but as it relates to your Mission Statement, you should prioritize only three.

If you have a retail store and sell hundreds of products, you can batch your economic priorities into categories. For instance, a priority such as "we will sell thirty-five bags of dog food each day" speaks to an economic priority that will drive overall growth. You may sell twenty different brands of dog food, but because you've batched sales into a category, your team can engineer the accomplishment of that objective. If you're behind on your goal, your team can create an end cap where you display the dog food or perhaps send out an email to customers who own dogs and inform them of their options.

What you'll find is that by clearly stating the mission of increasing up to three financial priorities, you and your team open a financial story loop that must be tended to in order to close. In other words, including financial priorities in your Mission Statement focuses your mission on the economic realities that will keep your business safe and allow you to grow.

Along with sales objectives, it's also okay to include lead measures that lead to sales. A lead measure is something like "X number of applications" or "X number of email addresses that will download our lead generator and enter into our sales funnel." While these are not direct financial objectives, they do lead to sales, so they're nearly as good as financial objectives. For instance, webinars, open houses, and keynote presentations all lead to sales if they are designed to lead to sales.

Where do we put the financial priorities in our Mission Statement? Right up front:

The first part of your Mission Statement will read: We will accomplish X. That "X" represents your three economic priorities.

For instance: We will sell one hundred units of X, three hundred units of Y, and fifty units of Z.

Or: We will help forty-two clients sell their houses, fifty-three clients buy new houses, and hold eighteen open houses.

It's that simple. All you have to do is identify three financial objectives that will move the business forward and include them in your Mission Statement.

To get the most out of your Mission Statement, your three economic priorities should:

- Be specific and measurable,
- Drive company revenue, and
- Drive company profit.

Will it drive revenue and profit to increase subscriptions by 20 percent? If so, that's a measurable statistic you can include in your Mission Statement.

Let's say you run a restaurant and want to be known for your incredible desserts. Great. Instead of saying "We will be known for our desserts," you will say "We will average forty-seven desserts per dinner segment each night." An economic objective like this will cause you and your team to start initiating efforts to hit your goal. If you're averaging only twenty desserts, your team can start asking each table if they'd like desert, or perhaps print up a separate dessert menu and bring it to each table just as they are wrapping up dinner. Again, if you include economic priorities in your Mission Statement, you and your team will start creating ways to hit those goals. If your Mission Statement is elusive, it will not spark the kind of creativity necessary to grow a business.

Why Should the Three Economic Priorities Be Measurable?

It's important the three financial priorities in your Mission Statement be measurable because it must be obvious whether or not you have accomplished your mission. If you exist to make customers happy, that's great, but that's also wildly anecdotal.

"Happy customers" is a difficult objective to measure. Instead of saying you want "happy customers," say you want "250 return customers within the next twenty-four months." Stating the economic priority in such a way that it can be measured allows you to engineer and execute a plan to accomplish that mission. If you fail, no problem: Identify why you missed the mark, adjust your plan, extend your deadline, and keep going.

Define three critical economic priorities for your business, and you'll have more money for payroll, benefits, and your growing business profit account that you can later use to make outside investments and grow your personal wealth.

What are the three critical economic priorities you want to include in your Mission Statement?

EXAMPLES:

A brewery: We will increase our distribution of beer to seventy-five more restaurants, four more grocery store chains, and twenty-seven bars by . . .

A magazine: We will increase our subscriber base to 22,000, our advertisers by 40 percent, and raise the average customer advertising investment to $22K by . . .

A consulting firm: We will serve thirty new clients, sell five new retainer packages, and receive 98 percent client satisfaction survey results during the period of . . .

Brainstorm Your Three Economic Priorities

Write part one of your Mission Statement with the following simple phrase:

WE WILL ACCOMPLISH:

———————————————————————————————

———————————————————————————————

———————————————————————————————

———————————————————————————————

Once you complete your mission statement you can transfer your statement to the Small Business Flight Plan.

Feel Free to Change Your Mission Statement in Real Time

Most large companies would be unable to change their Mission Statement in real time, but you do not run a large company. There's no reason you can't change your mission statement every couple of years.

Your Mission Statement is not a legal document; it is designed to create narrative traction and inspire action so you and your team don't lose the plot along the way. If your three economic priorities are not generating clarity and focus, change the statement. Simply gather your team and talk about what needs to change. In fact, we changed our three critical priorities several times before we dialed in the objectives that now drive our growth. Add to that our deadline is rarely further out than eighteen months, so our mission statement is edited and adjusted at least every eighteen months.

When should you change your Mission Statement? Simple. Change your Mission Statement under two circumstances: First, when you have accomplished all or part of your mission, and second, when you realize your Mission Statement isn't inspiring action. Continue to edit your Mission Statement until it inspires a mission, then let it ride.

Now that the team knows the economic priorities that serve as your destination and can help you create a flight plan, let's talk about increasing the urgency of your mission.

Mission Statement Part Two: Include a Deadline for Your Financial Priorities in Your Mission Statement

When storytellers and screenwriters want to make a story more interesting, they include a deadline. It's one thing that our hero wants to marry the woman he loves, but it's even better if the woman is getting married to his jerk of a brother in less than a week! When a story includes a deadline, it gets a lot more interesting.

In fact, one of the most popular television series of all time was based on a twenty-four-hour countdown clock slowly ticking down. Millions watched as Kiefer Sutherland attempted to stop the bad guys before the clock hit zero.

A ticking clock is an incredible device to increase you and your team's intensity as it relates to hitting those three financial objectives.

After you determine your three financial objectives, include the date those objectives must be accomplished by as the next part of your Mission Statement.

When you include a deadline, your Mission Statement will read something like this:

We will accomplish _____, _____, and _____ by _____.

Each of your three economic objectives should share the same deadline. The idea is to choose a date in which you can accomplish everything in your Mission Statement and then dream your Mission Statement up again to continue to inspire growth.

It's rare to see a deadline in a Mission Statement, which is yet another reason most Mission Statements are ineffective.

Deadlines help people understand that a project is urgent. The product must be on the shelves within twelve months. The debt must be paid off within three years. The new hire needs to be onboarded within ninety days.

All of this begs the question: What do we do when we reach the deadline? That's a great question. The answer is you either learn from the failure to accomplish the mission or celebrate the accomplishment of the mission. Then you edit your Mission Statement to make it relevant again.

How Much Time Should We Give Ourselves to Accomplish Our Mission?

It's not a bad idea to change the economic objectives along with the deadline every one or two years. If the deadline in your Mission Statement extends beyond two years, you're going to lose that sense of urgency.

Human beings tend to view their future lives as though those lives belong to somebody else. Humans may think about the future, but they live in the now and tend to concern themselves with how they feel today and, perhaps tomorrow, but not much further out than that.

A deadline that extends one to two years will not extend so far into the future that it loses its sense of importance.

EXAMPLES:

A brewery: We will increase our distribution of beer to seventy-five more restaurants, four more grocery store chains, and twenty-seven bars *by the end of the fiscal year.*

A magazine: We will increase our subscriber base to 22,000, our advertisers by 40 percent, and the average customer advertising investment to $22K *within two years.*

A consulting firm: We will serve thirty new clients, sell five new retainer packages, and receive 98 percent client satisfaction survey results *by December 31.*

Take some time either alone or with your team and decide upon a deadline to accomplish your three economic objectives. When you have decided upon a deadline, add it to your mission statement.

After you define up to three financial objectives and set a deadline, you will want to finish your Mission Statement by reminding yourself and your team why hitting these objectives matters. Let's answer the question "why?"

Mission Statement Part Three: Explain Why the Mission Matters

The Mission Statement "We will mow lawns for more than 300 families by the end of the year" is a good start, but to finish it off with a bang, add the why: "because everybody deserves to come home to a lawn they love."

This simple "because" addition gives you and your team a great reason to drive your mission forward and reminds you why you are in businesses in the first place. In fact, the "because" part of our Mission Statement *is* the actual mission. Without the "because," all you have is a goal and goals in and of themselves will not inspire your business into expansion and growth. A mission is much more important than a goal. A mission happens when we accept the challenge to improve the lives of our customers.

Here are two things your Mission Statement can include to turn your goals into a mission:

1. **A vision of a better world:** Tell us, specifically, how the world will be better if you accomplish the mission. What will people see? What will they feel?
2. **A counterattack against an injustice:** Tell us about the suffering people will no longer have to experience if you accomplish your mission. What broken thing will be restored?

When you include a because, your mission matters, and you and your team will be energized around that cause.

EXAMPLES:

A brewery: We will increase our distribution of beer to seventy-five more restaurants, four more grocery store chains, and twenty-seven bars by the end of the fiscal year *because everybody deserves access to their new favorite beer.*

A magazine: We will increase our subscriber base to 22,000, our advertisers by 40 percent, and the average customer advertising investment to $22K within two years *because good journalism can save the country.*

A consulting firm: We will serve thirty new clients, sell five new retainer packages, and receive 98 percent client satisfaction survey results by December 31 *because everybody deserves the help they need to grow a business.*

What's your because? What's the "why" of your mission? Close your Mission Statement with a good reason to take action and you and your team will do just that.

Put All Three Parts Together for the Perfect Mission Statement

Again, the Mission Statement should define up to three financial priorities, set a deadline, and describe the reason the mission matters. If you do this in your Mission Statement, your entire team will know what vision they are supposed to be advancing and why their work matters.

It may take some time for you to perfect your Mission Statement. Feel free to write it and edit it. Simply ask for grace from your team as, together, you change the priorities, the deadline, and the reason why until the Mission Statement creates narrative traction.

The point of the Mission Statement was never to check a box and have some meaningless words on a page. The point of the Mission Statement is to invite you and your team into a story that everybody finds engaging.

All storytellers workshop their plot lines to make them more interesting. Feel free to do the same with your Mission Statement.

When you finally have your Mission Statement nailed down, it's time to embed that mission into your own mind and the minds of everybody who will be working to accomplish the mission.

Once You Write Your Mission Statement, What Do You Do with It?

Another mistake leaders make with their Mission Statement is they write it, read it a couple times, and then file it away. At best, the Mission Statement is buried in small text on their website or perhaps in an HR brochure they hand to new employees.

If you and your team members can't remember the Mission Statement, you and your team members can't remember the mission.

Once you write your Mission Statement, you'll want to launch a communication campaign that helps you and your team take action on that statement. And we all know what it takes to remember something: repetition.

Here are four ways to help your team remember the mission:

1. Open your All-Staff Meetings by reading through the
    Mission Statement.
2. On a monthly or quarterly basis, acknowledge a team
    member for advancing the mission and tell their story
    as a way of highlighting the team member and the
    mission.
3. Ask potential hires to read the Mission Statement
    and write down why that mission is important
    to them.
4. Have the Mission Statement written on the wall
    of your place of business and make a production
    (and celebration) out of changing it as the mission
    shifts.

Again, the idea is to see your Mission Statement as the plot
line of a story and to remind your team of that story every chance
you get.

Once you write your Mission Statement, you are one-third of
the way toward creating the Guiding Principles that will serve as
the foundation of your company.

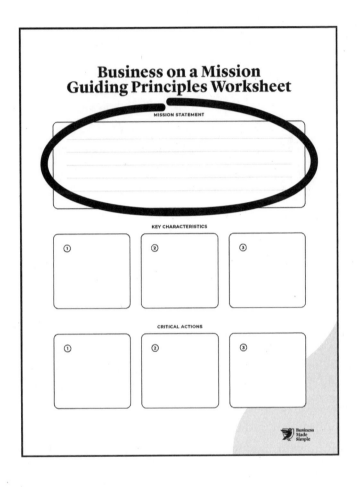

Access a digital, fillable version at SmallBusinessFlightPlan.com

Next, let's define the sort of people you are going to need to recruit (and become) in order to accomplish your mission. Let's define your Key Characteristics.

Once you complete your mission statement, transfer it to the Guiding Principles Worksheet in your Small Business Flight Plan.

STEP ONE: PART TWO

Define Your Key Characteristics

Almost every story you love is about a character or a group of characters who want something and have to overcome obstacles to get what they want. What we really love about those stories, though, is not that the hero gets what they want, it's that the hero transforms into a better version of themselves in order to get what they want.

Human beings love to watch other human beings transform into better versions of themselves. In fact, we are absolutely obsessed with people who transform. Whether we're watching a television show about somebody who has gotten into amazing physical shape or a documentary about an orphan kid who grew up to become president, we are inspired and motivated by the idea that we, too, can transform.

Humans are active, fluid, ever-changing beings. We learn and grow and transform the more we engage in the story of life.

But how do human beings transform? Why do they transform? What causes transformation?

Human beings transform when they want something that requires them to become a better version of themselves in order to attain that something. Whether we want healthy intimacy and realize we need to see a counselor or we want to climb a mountain and so set out to physically transform into a person who is capable of such a feat, we change when we fully engage in something that sits beyond our current capability.

In fact, when you wrote down your Mission Statement, you not only invited yourself and others into a story, you invited yourself and others to transform into the sort of people who could accomplish that mission.

In fact, what top talent wants more than anything else is to work for a business that will help them transform into a high-value professional. If your Mission Statement is aspirational, they will see that opportunity in your business.

You and your team will have to develop certain characteristics in order to achieve your mission. In your package of Guiding Principles, these characteristics are called Key Characteristics.

You can think of your Key Characteristics as "core values" if you like, but to me, they are even better than core values. Core values are great, but often words like "integrity" are too elusive to live out. Besides, "integrity" is a core value of being human. If you don't have integrity, you will likely end up in prison. Key Characteristics are more specific; they identify a specific set of skills or personality characteristics necessary to work for your company.

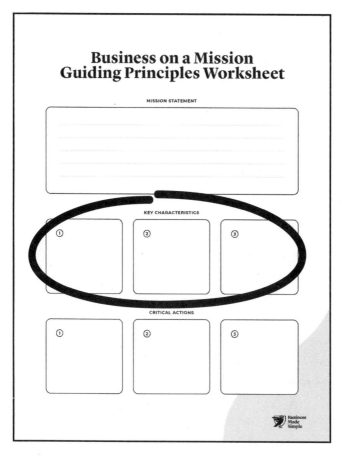

Access a digital, fillable version at SmallBusinessFlightPlan.com

For instance, if you are a software engineer, you may need team members who are obsessed with simplifying a user interface. If you are a pet store owner, you definitely want team members who love animals.

When you make your core values more specific by turning them into Key Characteristics, you better know what characteristics to develop in yourself and what characteristics to look for in new hires.

If you ask a potential hire if they have integrity, everybody will say, "Of course" The same thing will happen if you ask a pet store applicant if they love animals. But if you ask a potential new hire what they've done that demonstrates their love of animals, you'll be much more likely to find out whether or not you've got the right candidate.

Here are three questions to ask when determining your Key Characteristics:

1. What specific characteristics will each of us need in order to create (or sell) the products that solve our customers' problems?
2. What characteristics will we need to keep going when the challenges seem overwhelming?
3. What characteristics will we need to create a safe, encouraging culture?

When you define the Key Characteristics you will need to embody in order to accomplish your mission, you determine who you will need to transform into and what kind of people you will need to hire.

How Many Key Characteristics Should We List?

In order to accomplish your mission, you and the members of your team will likely need to embody a number of character traits. In fact, different departments may need to embody different Key Characteristics.

For purposes of simplifying our Guiding Principles, though, we're recommending you include only three Key Characteristics in your list. These three Key Characteristics should be specific enough to guide your hiring decisions but universal enough to be true for everybody in your organization.

Here's a great example of some Key Characteristics for a local restaurant:

1. We love people and enjoy serving them.
2. We are obsessed with great-tasting food.
3. We are calm under pressure.

Notice how specific these Key Characteristics are. The restaurant did not choose to say, "We are customer oriented." They said, "We love people and enjoy serving them." Because they defined exactly what sort of attitude to have when interacting with customers, their team members know how they are supposed to act. Anybody can be optimistic and still put people off, but if we are "positive when interacting with people," we will hardly ever put people off.

Equally, if we are obsessed with great-tasting food, every member of the team is reminded to make sure the ingredients are fresh, that food is served in a timely manner, and that any plate that doesn't look right goes back to the chef for review. Why? If we are obsessed with great-tasting food, we are always learning and growing and discovering new ways of making food taste better.

Finally, if the restaurant is going to grow, team members will need to stay calm under pressure. This is a big one. This invites team members to learn and grow and always become the sort of people who are calm under pressure. This Key Characteristic defines an aspirational identity. If the pressure gets intense, the leader can remind team members to remain calm under pressure—a characteristic that will no doubt become a defining attribute of the team. Not only this, but if they are developing the ability to be calm under pressure, they are finding better ways to organize the kitchen, expedite orders, and give individual attention to their guests even while the restaurant is buzzing around them.

Most importantly, though, these three characteristics contribute to the restaurant hitting its financial objectives. Think about it, if you walked into a restaurant with a staff that was incredibly positive, then they served food that tasted amazing, and they were never so overwhelmed that they failed to give you individual attention, wouldn't you go back? Of course. That restaurant is going to grow, without question, because they defined the sort of people they would need to become in order to accomplish their mission and then actively began to transform into those kinds of people.

Here are some examples of the Key Characteristics different kinds of businesses could choose:

EXAMPLES:

Network Marketing Product Rep:
1. Loves connecting with people,
2. Believes their product can change lives, and
3. Is always resilient.

Financial Advisor:
1. Always puts the customers first,
2. Can clearly explain complicated investments, and
3. Enjoys helping families leave a legacy.

Consultant:

1. Terrific at turning knowledge into practical frameworks,
2. Loves networking with people, and
3. Is obsessed with solving clients' problems.

Now it's time for you to define your Key Characteristics. What three characteristics will you and your teammates need to embody in order to accomplish your mission?

Brainstorm the Key Characteristics you and your team members will need to embody to accomplish the mission. When you decide on the top three, transfer them to your Small Business Flight Plan.

KEY CHARACTERISTICS:

_____

_____

_____

Now that you know your three economic priorities along with what kind of people you need to become to reach your financial objectives, let's talk about what actions we need to take in order to live the mission.

STEP ONE:
PART THREE
Determine Your Critical Actions

C reating a package of Guiding Principles can be one of the most inspirational exercises you perform as a small-business owner. It's an amazing experience to sit and dream about what the future can be. It would be a big mistake, though, to stop at dreaming. In order to achieve your mission, you're going to have to take action.

Very few Guiding Principle frameworks include Critical Actions in their offering, but I believe Critical Actions are nearly as important, or even more important than Key Characteristics. If we don't embody the mission in action, we will never make an impact.

In the Critical Action section of your Guiding Principles Worksheet, you're going to define three actions every member of your team can take nearly every day that will move the business toward its three financial objectives.

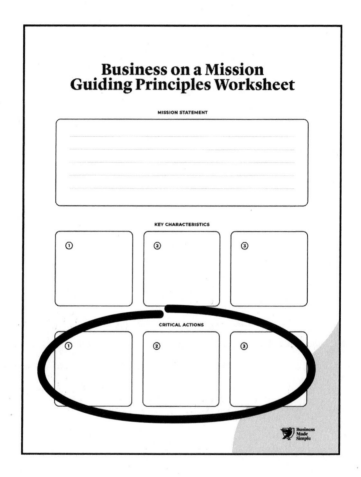

Access a digital, fillable version at SmallBusinessFlightPlan.com

If you're a solo-preneur, this exercise is simple. All you need to do is define three things that, if done every day, will automatically propel you toward your mission. If you've got a few team members, you're looking for three things every one of you can do and the same goes for those of us with thirty or forty or even four hundred team members.

When defining Critical Actions, you're looking to create habits that move the mission forward. If nearly everybody on your team develops three habits that directly affect the bottom line, the business will almost certainly thrive.

What Sort of Actions Should Be Defined as Critical?

Your three Critical Actions should have two things in common:

1. Nearly everybody on the team can do them, and
2. They should directly affect the forward movement that will assist the accomplishment of your mission.

Let's go back to our restaurant example. If everybody on the team made a habit of asking people if they've tried "our amazing desserts," there's no question the restaurant would sell more desserts. Also, if they took turns cleaning the bathroom every hour, the entire restaurant would feel more clean. Those two Critical Actions would affect the restaurant's revenue and the overall customer experience. Not only that, but if one of the Critical Actions was that the team took turns bringing sweet tea to people waiting in line to get in, even more customers would rave about the restaurant.

The word "nearly" is important when I say "nearly" every employee could take "nearly" every Critical Action every day. The truth is if a chef is back in the kitchen, they likely won't be handing out sweet tea. But even the chef, when walking through the dining room and talking to families sitting at tables, could ask them if they'd tried the amazing desserts and then answer a few questions about the German chocolate cake.

Use Your Critical Actions to Create a Terrific Culture

When you say thank you to any team member at Chick-fil-A, they respond by saying "my pleasure." The idea that it's a pleasure to serve customers is demonstrated through the Critical Action of saying "my pleasure" and, as such, creates a culture of positive service to guests.

Your Critical Actions can go a long way in creating a culture, especially if most of your team members are performing the Critical Actions every day.

When people take the same actions together, it creates a kind of bond that results in a tribe. Watch any college football game and you'll see the Critical Actions fans take in the stands. Whether it's a certain cheer, a certain dance to a certain song at a certain time in the game, or just a loud booing of the ref when they don't like the call, these actions create a tribal bond and make a group of people feel like one.

Besides creating a bond, the Critical Actions that are taken by you and nearly every member of your team amplify whatever message your actions are broadcasting to the world. If a real estate office decides one of their Critical Actions is to "sign a thank-you card" for every client that buys a home, they are amplifying the message that they care about their clients and are happy for their big new move. This simple Critical Action will do many things. It lets everybody in the office know that another home has been sold and reminds them that lives are changed every time a customer moves into their new home. It is also another pleasing and thoughtful interaction with customers that will lead to word-of-mouth recommendations for that particular real estate office.

Test Out Your Critical Actions Until You Find Three That Fit

Don't overthink your Critical Actions. If you're looking for the "right actions" to take, you're likely going to get frustrated. The truth is there are a thousand great Critical Actions that will work to grow your small business. You're simply looking for three Critical Actions that have a terrific impact so you can turn them into habits and use them to propel the company forward.

A Critical Action could be as simple as "we have a Stand-up meeting every morning in which we talk about the day's goals" or "we review our client list every day and identify any special needs they may have before they come in." If you think about it, those two Critical Actions would lead to incredible success. If you identify your goals every single day, you're more likely to hit those goals, and if you identify your clients' special needs, you're more likely to create a memorable connection when they come in, which will lead to return visits and positive word of mouth.

Feel free to test out your Critical Actions and replace any that aren't getting traction with you and your team. The process may take a little time, but soon you'll find you and your team are performing three Critical Actions that are moving the company forward and those actions are quickly being turned into habits that define your culture.

EXAMPLES:

Bakery:
1. We offer a sample to everybody who comes in the front door.
2. We check the expiration dates on all ingredients in the pantry.
3. We clean our personal workspaces every hour on the hour.

Manufacturing Company:
1. We wear our hard hats and gloves at all times.
2. We keep a clean workspace.
3. We review yesterday's progress and write down our goals at the beginning of every shift.

Solo-preneur's Online Learning Platform:
1. I call every new customer and thank them for their order.
2. I create one new Instagram post per day offering terrific free value.
3. I fill out my daily planner every morning and decide on what content I need to create that day.

Take some time and identify three Critical Actions you and your team can take that will directly contribute to the achievement of your Mission Statement.

Brainstorm your Critical Actions and when you've decided on three, add them to your Guiding Principles Worksheet in your Small Business Flight Plan.

YOUR THREE CRITICAL ACTIONS:

_____

_____

_____

On the following pages you will see examples of how three businesses completed their Business on a Mission Guiding Principles Worksheet.

B2C Example: Wedding Cake Bakery

Business on a Mission
Guiding Principles Worksheet

MISSION STATEMENT

We will sell 250 wedding cakes, promote one new flavor every month, and attract 2,500 new leads by the end of the calendar year because everyone deserves to have a cake they can show off at their wedding.

KEY CHARACTERISTICS

① Creative

② Learns one new decorating technique per month

③ Keeps their personal station clean and organized

CRITICAL ACTIONS

① Greets everyone with a smile and a sample

② Learns new decorating techniques

③ First response to a challenge is "Thank you, we'll find a way."

Business
Made
Simple

Access a digital, fillable version at SmallBusinessFlightPlan.com

B2B Example: Cybersecurity Solutions

Business on a Mission
Guiding Principles Worksheet

MISSION STATEMENT

We will conduct 100 new security audits, create security packages for 50 new clients, and retain 250 monthly subscribers by the end of the year because defending your business against cyber attacks shouldn't feel overwhelming.

KEY CHARACTERISTICS

① Think like a hacker

② Strong sense of justice

③ Competitive and likes to win

CRITICAL ACTIONS

① Turns their work in on time

② Goes above and beyond their job description

③ Fills out their Department Stand-up every day

Business Made Simple

Access a digital, fillable version at SmallBusinessFlightPlan.com

Nonprofit Example: Home Building

Business on a Mission Guiding Principles Worksheet

MISSION STATEMENT

We will recruit financial sponsors to build 50 homes, find 50 families to qualify for a new home, and sign with five Diamond Level corporate partners by the end of the fiscal year because every family deserves to feel secure with a roof over their heads and food on their table.

KEY CHARACTERISTICS

① Pays attention to families in need

② Has an eye for excellence in the building and development space

③ Shows up on time and prepared

CRITICAL ACTIONS

① Shares our mission with everyone they meet

② Memorizes families' stories and shares them

③ Boldly asks potential donors to join our mission

Business Made Simple

Access a digital, fillable version at SmallBusinessFlightPlan.com

What to Do with Your Guiding Principles after You Create Them

Now that you've got your Mission Statement, your Key Characteristics, and your Critical Actions defined, you can put them all on your Guiding Principles Worksheet.

Here are some things you can do with your Guiding Principles so you and your team are more likely to live them and accomplish your mission:

- Review them weekly at your All-Staff Meeting.
- Ask for "shout-outs" in your All-Staff Meeting to praise team members who've lived out your Key Characteristics.
- Have your Guiding Principles artistically painted on a wall in your place of business.
- Review and edit them in a special, biannual meeting with your leadership team.
- Announce any new edits or changes to your Guiding Principles with great fanfare.
- Create videos that explain (and demonstrate) your Guiding Principles so new hires can review them.
- Include your Guiding Principles in any recruiting collateral.

Congratulations, now that you've created your Guiding Principles using the Business on a Mission Framework, you've got a foundation on which to build your small business. Providing a compelling vision, Key Characteristics, and Critical Actions will transform you and your leadership team into trusted guides who are positioned to help everybody on the team accomplish the mission and experience a victory.

After you employ the Business on a Mission Framework and feel comfortable moving forward, start working on Step Two: Clarify Your Marketing Message.

2

Marketing

STEP TWO:
The Right Engine

*Clarify Your Marketing Message
Using the StoryBrand Framework*

Step Two Will Help You Solve These Problems:

- You aren't sure how to talk about your products so they sell.
- Your website and marketing collateral isn't converting to sales.
- Customers aren't spreading the word about your brand.
- Your social media doesn't have a controlling idea.
- You have not created a loyal brand following.
- When you talk about your products, people just get confused.

If you've read my book Building a StoryBrand, *this is the only chapter in the book that will be review material. The rest of the book will be new to you. That said, don't skip Step Two. Reviewing and refining your marketing engine is key to increasing thrust and getting the plane off the ground.*

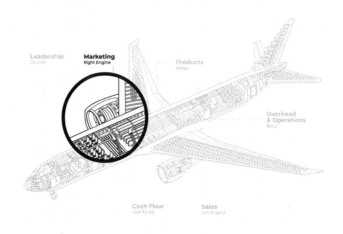

· · ·

The first thing nearly everybody does when they start a small business is to hire somebody to design a logo and brand colors. They love their logo and so they put it on a baseball cap and coffee cup and book bag and give the swag out to friends and family. The problem is, having your logo printed on some swag does not increase sales. Getting your brand right without doing actual marketing is like painting the side of an airplane that is not yet engineered to fly.

How many sales does a good logo and friendly swag lead to? Usually none. In fact, the only people who make money off your logo and coffee cup investment are the people who design the logo and the company that sold you the coffee cup.

Creating a logo and choosing brand colors are very important, of course, but there are other things that are more important. Communicating to potential customers that your product will solve a problem they are struggling with and then asking those potential customers to place an order is infinitely more important than putting your logo on swag.

If you've already created your logo and identified your brand style guide, don't worry. That's just one more step you won't have to take later. For now, though, let's get your plane moving forward. Let's get some cash flowing through your cash register.

The next two steps represent the right and left engines of your airplane. The right engine represents marketing; the left engine represents sales. Because an engine's job is to create thrust and move the airplane forward, we are going to talk about how both engines can move the wings (products) of your airplane fast enough to create lift.

Clarify Your Message and Customers Will Listen

Our marketing effort will focus on one clear objective: to explain what our products have to offer in such clear, simple language that everybody understands why they should buy our products and is motivated to do so.

This may sound like some form of manipulation but marketing should not be about manipulation. It should be about clarity. If you manipulate people, you might sell them something once.

But if you clearly explain what you offer, you create trust and repeat business.

When we talk about marketing, we're often talking about our website, lead generators, advertising, and perhaps some signage, brochures, and/or flyers. Those are important pieces of marketing collateral, but the truth is the heart of your marketing is embodied in the words you use on those websites, advertisements, and signage.

Sadly, most small businesses think more about how their marketing will look rather than what their marketing will say. This will never work. Why? Because the reason customers place orders is not because a brand design is attractive, it's because they read or hear words that make them want to place orders.

In the marketing step that helps you build the right engine of your airplane, we are going to get your marketing engine moving by creating some simple Soundbites you can repeat in your marketing collateral. The sharper your words and the more often you use them, the faster your airplane will go and the more lift you will achieve.

This is where a BrandScript comes into play. A BrandScript is made up of seven "talking points" you can use to invite customers into a story in which they buy your product to solve one of their problems and, hopefully, live happily ever after.

In this chapter I am going to guide you through the process of creating those talking points.

When you're done creating a BrandScript, you'll have powerful words you can use on your website, in your lead generators and emails, and even in your presentations. If you use the framework I am about to introduce you to, you will have the words you need to get more customers interested in your products.

Your Small Business Will Be Built with Words

When we think about building our small business, we likely think about the time we will have to put in, the money we will have to invest, the team members we will need to hire, and the physical products we will have to create.

One area we often overlook is the words we will use to describe our products. The truth is our business will grow because we've used words that make people want to buy our products. If we don't know how to talk about our products, our business will not grow.

The words you use to talk about your products matter. When people visit your website, they read words about your products. Those words can entice them or confuse them. Sales will only happen when those words entice them to place orders. When people pick up your product, they will read the words on the packaging. When customers read your emails or scroll through your social media, they will read words that either pique their interest or confuse them and turn them off. Due to your words, they will either be drawn into a story in which they play the hero and use your product to solve a problem, or they will find your product uninteresting and move on.

The point is this: Your brand is built with words.

So what kind of words do we need to use to attract people to our products and encourage them to place orders?

If you want to use words to help people understand why your products matter, remember two primary ideas:

1. People are only attracted to information that helps them survive and thrive, and

2. People, for the most part, only listen to ideas that are communicated simply.

Tell People How You Can Help Them Survive and Thrive

The first mistake brands make when it comes to talking about their products is they fail to focus on the aspects of their offer that will help people survive and thrive.

Human beings are designed to survive. In fact, that's the dominant job of the human brain: It scans the environment for information, tools, and connections that will keep itself alive. This means the entire time you're walking around on the Earth, you are looking for things and people who can help you stay alive (and thrive) and mostly ignoring the rest. Survival is the dominant objective of every person you have ever met, including you.

If you want to sell more products, talk about the aspects of your products that will help people survive and thrive. Nobody cares whether your grandfather started the company, but they definitely care whether or not your product can solve a problem that is keeping them up at night. When we talk about the aspects of our products that will help people survive and thrive, they will pay attention. And if we don't, they won't.

Don't Make the Customer Think Too Much

The next thing we have to do if we want people to buy our products is use simple, plain language. If we don't communicate clearly, we will be ignored. Customers are constantly scanning their environment for things and people who can help them survive. But because they are so bombarded with information, they don't have a great deal of time to study anything that doesn't immediately pique their survival instinct.

Your brain filters out nearly everything, processing only the information that will help you survive and thrive. This means most marketing messages are entirely ignored. If your brain didn't filter out information it doesn't need, your life would be entirely unmanageable. You'd walk into a coffee shop, stop to study the hinge on the door, and a few hours later still be standing there asking what kind of grease, if any, is used to keep the hinge from squeaking. Why? Because the filter in your brain that says *you don't need that information to survive* is missing.

Most of the "interesting" things around us in life go completely ignored. We tend to ignore almost anything we do not need to survive. The problem is, if you don't position your products as tools people can use to thrive, your products will then be ignored.

What do I mean by survive? I mean save money, make money, find rest, feel better, connect with more people, create a memory with loved ones, take care of ourselves, find love, be entertained, rest and recharge, eat, defend ourselves, and so on.

So, if the two things we need to do to sell more products are 1) associate our products with the survival of our customer, and 2) use short, simple Soundbites, what sort of messages should we use in our marketing? The answer is simple: Associate our products with our customers' survival in such short, simple Soundbites that people don't have to think too much to understand why they should buy them.

In other words, don't tell people about how your great grandmother started the company or how you've got a terrific, "great places to work" metric or that you are building a new building or any of the stuff that is all about *your* survival but has nothing to do with your *customer's* survival.

Your customers have an innate filter; if you are not talking about how you can help them survive and thrive, they will tune you out.

Use Story to Create Short, Simple Soundbites

To create short, simple Soundbites that break through the nearly impenetrable filter of the human brain, we're going to use the incredible power of story. There is nothing that will get your sales and marketing engines turning faster than story. Nothing.

One of the biggest challenges in marketing is to get people to stop tuning us out and actually pay attention long enough for us to communicate why they should buy our product. And the challenge is real.

Did you know the average human brain spends 30 percent of its time daydreaming? When we're sitting in traffic, we begin to daydream. When we're reading a book, it's all we can do to force ourselves to not daydream.

Daydreaming, it turns out, is a survival mechanism. When you daydream, your brain is saying, "There's nothing here that can help me survive or thrive so I'm going to conserve calories in case I need the mental energy later."

One of the few things that can make you stop daydreaming for an extended period of time is story. When we sit down to watch a movie or read a novel, our brains lock into the story, and we will pay attention for hours. We've all had the experience of starting a Netflix series only to realize, hours later, we've been sitting on the couch all day. Story is so compelling we cannot turn away.

So, if story causes us to pay attention, how can we harness the power of story to generate interest in our brand and our products?

Luckily, story is built on age-old formulas. Storytellers of all sorts have been using these formulas for centuries to capture their audiences' attention. The same storytelling used in ancient Greece is now used in virtual reality videogaming.

When you create your StoryBrand BrandScript, you create seven categories of Soundbites that, if repeated in your marketing collateral, will help you invite customers into a story and generate more revenue for your brand. The StoryBrand Framework is a scaled-down version of the formulas storytellers have been using for ages. It's worked for them, and it will work for you.

In the first step, you used the Business on a Mission Framework to invite yourself and your team into a story; now you'll use the StoryBrand Framework to invite customers into a story that solves their problems and changes their lives.

The StoryBrand Seven-Part Framework

The StoryBrand Framework has been used by more than 700,000 business leaders to clarify their message and generate more thrust in their marketing engine. While it's been used for many Fortune 500 companies, it's mostly been used by small-business owners like yourself because it has an incredible power to clearly communicate your value offer to the public.

The framework will explain the seven plot points of a good story and deliver seven Soundbites you can use in your marketing. To clarify your message, use the seven Soundbites that invite customers into a story on your website or landing page, in your lead generators, nurture and sales emails, and presentations.

If you're not sure how to talk about your products and services in a way that makes customers want to place orders, that is about to change.

The StoryBrand Seven-Part Framework looks like this:

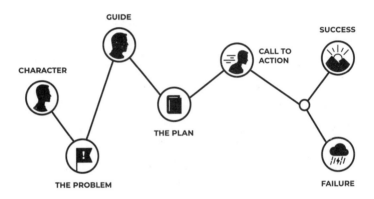

When you are finished with Step Two, you'll have words you can use to tell people about what you sell and why what you sell will help them survive and thrive.

StoryBrand Element One: A Character Who Wants Something

A story starts when we meet a character who wants something. The hero wants to disarm the bomb. The athlete wants to win the championship. The couple wants to get married.

When the central character wants something, the audience starts to pay attention because a story question is posited: Will the hero get what they want?

This is the first thing to remember in your marketing: To get attention, you need to identify something your potential customer wants and then talk about it in your marketing collateral. Do they want their pet to live a long and happy life? Do they want an electric car that will go farther on a single charge? Do they want to send their kids to a school where they get more attention from teachers?

When we start talking about the things our customers feel they need in order to survive and thrive, they start paying attention.

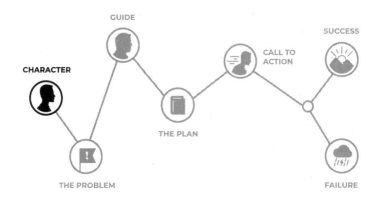

The key here is to be specific. If you're a marriage counselor, you might be tempted to say something like, "Our clients want to be happy at home," but this is too vague. Without context, this statement could be coming from a furniture company, a home security company, or even a swimming pool company. Instead, you might say something like, "Our clients want to rekindle the love they once shared with their spouse."

The more specific you are, the more likely you are to open a story loop in your customer's mind.

ANSWER THIS QUESTION: What does your customer need from your small business?

_____

Once you identify something specific your customers want, you've got the first Soundbite you can use in your marketing collateral.

Why does this Soundbite lead to sales? Because once we identify something our potential customers want, we've opened a story loop in their mind. The only way they can close that story loop is to buy our product or service.

But there's a problem: Just because we've identified something our potential customers want doesn't mean they will place an order. Plenty of people want things and don't buy them. They either talk themselves out of the purchase or get busy doing other things. In order to convince people they need your product or service, you must open that story loop a little wider.

StoryBrand Element Two: Must Overcome a Conflict

In stories, heroes do not get what they want right away. If they did, the story would be over in the first few pages. If a man wants to marry his high school sweetheart, and then he asks her to marry him, and then she says yes, and then they live happily ever after, we've got the most boring love story of all time.

Instead of getting what they want right away, heroes have to overcome enormous challenges. The man wants to marry his high school sweetheart but, sadly, she's in love with his brother who is a serious jerk—only she doesn't know it. He can't tell her that his brother is a jerk because, in doing so, he will cause tension in his family. So what does he do? How does he get through all this and hopefully end up with the woman of his dreams? Now that's a story question.

Conflict is what makes a story interesting. While none of us wants conflict in real life, we love it in stories. If you pause a movie at any point, you'll likely be looking at a hero who is up against serious problems. The hero is either emotionally wrought or in physical peril for the entire story. Storytellers add conflict because human beings identify with conflict. If you think about it, every human being is constantly trying to overcome a problem in their lives. Conflict makes us pay attention to the story. We wonder if the hero is going to get what they want. And when we see a character on the screen overcome conflict, we feel a sense of hope that we can overcome conflict too.

To create Soundbites that make people want to buy our products, we've got to talk about the problems our customers are dealing with and how our products solve said problems. When we talk about our customer's problems, our marketing works better and our airplane surges forward.

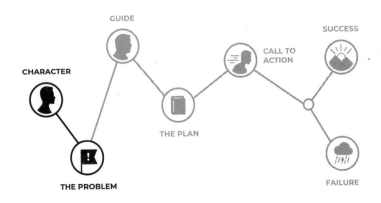

Here's the point: People only buy products and services to solve problems. If you talk about the problems your customers experience (that your product solves) you are further opening the story loop that they must buy your product to solve.

ANSWER THIS QUESTION: What are some of the problems your products help your customers overcome?

Now you have the second Soundbite you can use in your marketing collateral.

Of course, not all customers are going to be so quick to part with their money. We can still do more. Once we've identified what our customer wants and can speak clearly about the pain they experience because they've not yet bought our product, it's time to enter into their story and help them understand the solutions we offer.

StoryBrand Element Three: Meets a Guide

In stories, heroes need help to overcome their challenges. In fact, while we think of heroes as strong and capable, they are anything but. They are usually weak, ill-equipped, afraid, filled with self-doubt, and in desperate need of help. It's not until the final pages of the story that the hero is revealed as a transformed character capable of accomplishing their task.

So who helps the hero win the day? The guide.

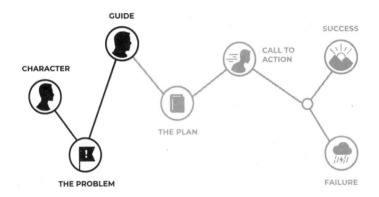

In stories, an often mysterious, strong, and capable character shows up to help the hero along their journey. This character is called the guide.

Mr. Miyagi is the guide for Daniel in *The Karate Kid*. Gandalf guides Frodo Baggins to help him destroy the ring in The Lord of the Rings series. Mary Poppins guides the children and their parents in the movie *Mary Poppins*.

Without guides, heroes would be lost. Without guides, heroes would never be able to overcome their problems.

Arguably the most important point in the entire StoryBrand Framework is this: Never play the hero; always play the guide.

Many small-business leaders make the mistake of positioning themselves as the hero in the story. They talk about how they created their product or how good their sales are or how long they've been in business, but customers aren't interested in your businesses. What they're interested in is whether or not you can help them solve a problem.

It's a mistake, then, as a leader or a small-business owner to position yourself as the hero. Heroes aren't looking for other heroes. Heroes are looking for guides who can help them.

When you position yourself as a guide, potential customers recognize you as somebody who can help them. When you position yourself as a hero, customers ignore you. You literally become invisible.

There are two things you need to do to position yourself as a guide.

The first thing you need to do is express empathy. Guides care more about the success of the hero than they do about their own success. The key words here are that "they care."

In your marketing collateral, you want to express empathy with the pain your potential customers are experiencing. Saying things like "We know how it feels to struggle with . . ." goes a long way in positioning you as a guide.

Remember, hero customers are afraid, ill equipped, frustrated, and in need of help, which is why they are looking for somebody who understands their dilemma.

In your marketing collateral, include statements of empathy so your customers recognize you as the guide who cares about their frustrations and pain.

The second thing you need to do to position yourself as a guide is demonstrate authority. By authority, I mean you've got to demonstrate that you actually know how to help your hero customers overcome their challenge and win the day.

It's not enough that you care about your customers; you also have to be able to lead them with competence. Have you helped hundreds of people overcome the problem your customer is dealing with? Have you created a technology that makes overcoming the challenge easier? Have you won awards for the work you've done? What can you say to your customer that will give them confidence you can help them solve their problems?

Statements like "We have helped thousands of people just like you overcome X . . ." or "Our award-winning technology has been featured in dozens of magazines . . ." let customers know you are proficient at solving their problem.

Many people think "not playing the hero" means that you cannot talk about yourself in your marketing collateral but this isn't true. You actually can talk about yourself. You can talk about how much you care about the customer's problem and you can talk about how competent you are at solving that problem.

When you express empathy and demonstrate authority, you position yourself as the guide in your customer's life. When customers know that you care about their problem and can help them get out of their jam, they seek you out for help.

There are two Soundbites you want to include in your marketing collateral that will help position you as a guide for potential customers. Those two Soundbites are:

EXPRESS EMPATHY:

_____

_____

DEMONSTRATE AUTHORITY:

_____

_____

Use these Soundbites in your marketing collateral and more customers will pay attention.

Once you position yourself as the guide your customers have been looking for, they will likely want to place an order. In fact, with just these three narrative elements in your marketing message, your right engine will work more efficiently and your revenue will increase. That said, many customers still won't place orders. It's true they recognize your product as a tool they can use to solve their problem and they respect you as the guide, but some of your customers are going to be risk averse. They're going to want to think about it for a while.

So how can we help them take that risky move, feel more comfortable, and hit the "buy now" button? We will give them a plan.

StoryBrand Element Four: Who Gives Them a Plan

Customers do not want to walk into the unknown. And even though you've identified something they want, have empathized with their problems, and have even demonstrated you can help them solve their problems, some still aren't going to make a purchase.

Why? They're at that point when they have to put skin in the game, and that's risky.

To you, making a purchase seems like the obvious next move. You've got a solution to their problem. You're experienced in helping people solve that problem. It's worked for plenty of other people. So why isn't the customer placing an order?

To your customer, though, the view is very different. They feel as though your solution is on the other side of a rushing river. They hear the water flowing thirty or forty feet downstream into a waterfall. If they try to cross that river, they could slip and fall, hit their head on a rock, and go floating right over the top of that waterfall.

That's absurd, of course. There's no danger in buying your product. You and I know it works. But the customer doesn't. To us, it's a sure thing. To them, it's a risk.

What do you do to help the customer gain more confidence that they won't be wasting their money? You place large stones in that river that act as stepping-stones. When the customer sees there is a clear path to cross the river, they become much more likely to place an order.

We all know how it feels to want to buy something but have a sense of unease about pulling the trigger. What we need to provide for the customer is baby steps. The stones you will place in the river represent a three- or four-step plan. When you give your customer a three- or four-step plan, they are much more likely to place an order.

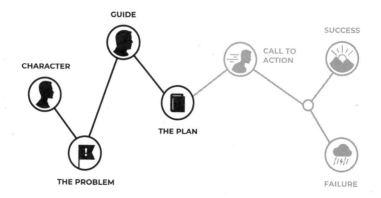

For the record, three-step plans work well; four-step plans work almost as well; five-step plans hardly work at all. A plan exists to let the customer know the journey from their problem to your solution will be easy. When you include five or more steps, you're actually saying the journey is difficult. Keep the plan easy, and your customer will feel safety and comfort and will start taking steps toward a purchase.

Instead of asking a customer to go ahead and make an offer on a house, for example, what if you said, "Let's do this safely. Let's contact the bank to make sure you qualify for the amount you'll need, then let's place an offer. If the house appraises at the right price, you can buy the house and move in."

Did you catch those three steps?

Making a big purchase like buying a house is risky business. When we offer three or four baby steps to our customers, they'll feel more comfortable moving ahead.

The product you sell doesn't have to be big and expensive to benefit from a plan, either. You can use a three-step plan to sell a pair of shoes: 1) Order the shoes, 2) Try them on at home,

3) Ship them back if they don't fit. You can do the same when selling a service: 1) Sign up for our HVAC maintenance program, 2) Get regular checkups and filter replacements, and 3) Never worry about your HVAC system again.

Another way to look at the plan in the story you are inviting customers into is that it "lifts the fog."

When customers are facing the prospect of loss, they get worried. They may not know they are worried, but when money is on the line, they are certainly worried. The idea of placing an order, for your customer, means they could lose their money, their self-respect, their sense that the world is trustworthy and so on. Imagine being a lonely hero having to walk into a dark forest in order to accomplish your task. As you look into the forest, you can only see a few feet into the forest because there is a dense fog drifting slowly and eerily thorough the trees.

When you present a plan to the customer, you essentially "lift the fog" so they can see much more of the terrain they will be venturing into.

When you break down the process into three or four steps, customers can see farther into the forest. For instance, instead of a financial advisor saying, "Let's get together and make a plan for your future," they could say, "I work with clients in three phases. First we assess where you want to go in life. Then, I put together a plan for you. Then, if you decide to move forward, we work together to execute that plan."

A three-step plan like this essentially tells the customer what the future looks like if they work with you, lifting the fog.

When a customer browses your website and becomes interested in placing an order, it's the plan that lets them know making a purchase is simple, safe, and easy. Including a plan on your landing page, in your emails, and in your sales presentations will cause a greater percentage of people to place an order.

Schedule a
free intake call

Get your
custom plan

Grow your
business

Ever walked into a CarMax car lot? The behemoth car dealership includes three-step plans for everything from buying a car to selling your car to buying a warranty for a car. These plans provide a mental map customers need to take in order to solve their problem.

ANSWER THIS QUESTION: What three or four steps do your customers need to take in order to buy your product and solve their problem?

_____

_____

When you use this three-step plan in your marketing collateral, your sales will increase.

Now that our customer is ready to place an order and we've given them a clear, simple path to take, let's encourage them to take a step. Let's call them to action!

StoryBrand Element Five: And Calls Them to Action

At this point in the story we are inviting customers into, they're ready to place an order. Some customers may even be so excited they call you to ask how they can purchase your product or service. Many customers, though, will not. They will wait for you to ask them to place the order. And if you don't ask them, they will walk away wishing you would have because they really, really wanted to give you their money in exchange for the solution you had to their problem.

It's a strange phenomenon, I agree, but it's a phenomenon all the same: People don't tend to do things unless you ask them to do things. And making a purchase is one of those things.

So what do you do about it? Call your customers to action with confidence.

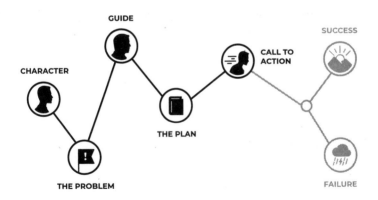

In stories, heroes are often lethargic. They did not ask to be thrown into this story, after all. Remember, they are ill equipped, filled with self-doubt, and in need of help. They just want all this mayhem to end so they can get back to the shire where life is comfortable!

Guides often have to challenge heroes to take action in order to help them resolve their problem. Leave the shire. Climb the mountain. Throw the punch. Go and win the heart of the person you love. Get moving!

What does this mean for our small business? It means we need to call our customers to action. We need to tell them it's time to place an order.

In our marketing collateral, this means there should be a "buy now" button on our website. In fact, there should be many "buy now" buttons and they should flow down the page in every section of our website. They should be bright, bold buttons. In fact, the "buy now" buttons should be the obvious buttons to press on your website.

Think of the "buy now" button on your website as a cash register. In a physical retail store, you'd never hide the cash register. You'd want customers to know where to bring their selection so they can make a purchase. The same is true on your website. Make your cash registers easy to find, click, and use.

If the buttons don't say "buy now," they should say something direct like "schedule an appointment" or "call today."

Many small-business leaders don't like to be pushy when it comes to marketing their products and services, but I assure you, very few small-business owners come off as pushy. In fact, most small-business owners make the opposite mistake: They are too passive in their calls to action. When we use language like "get started" or "learn more" we sound as though we don't believe in our products enough to encourage customers to place an order.

A customer wants to know you believe in your product and you are certain it can solve their problem.

Let's give customers something they can accept or reject in our marketing collateral. Let's call them to action. Let's ask them to make a purchase.

ANSWER THIS QUESTION: What will the main call to action be on your website and in your marketing collateral?

_____

_____

When you have clear calls to action in your marketing collateral, your sales will increase all the more.

Now that we've included strong calls to action in our marketing collateral, let's wrap up the story by including stakes.

To make the story you are inviting customers into interesting, customers need to know what can be won or lost based on whether or not they place an order. When we tell customers what they will get or what it will cost them if they do not buy from us, they are much, much more likely to place an order.

A good story needs stakes!

StoryBrand Element Six: So the Hero Can Avoid Failure

A good story needs stakes. Something must be won or lost based on whether or not the hero accomplishes the task at hand. Will the hero marry his sweetheart, or will she marry the evil brother and cause him to live heartbroken forever? Will the lawyer win the case and get justice for the entire town, or will all those people continue to suffer?

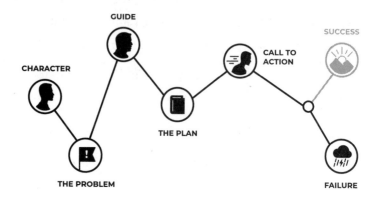

In a story, the audience is often reminded of what can be won or lost if the hero does or does not take action. We want to do the same in our marketing.

The two categories we will create Soundbites for in order to add stakes to the story are *failure* and *success*. If the customer does not buy our product or service, their story will end in failure, but if they do, their story will end in success.

In this section of our BrandScript, we want to create a talking point about what we are helping our customer avoid. People are motivated to avoid discomfort just as much (if not more) than they are motivated to seek comfort. Remember, human beings are problem solvers and are always trying to figure out how to avoid frustration and pain. When we remind them that our product keeps them away from frustration and pain, they become more motivated to buy.

Does the mattress you sell help customers overcome their backaches? Make sure to tell them that or, better, include that language in the signage next to the mattress itself or in the descriptive copy on your website. Does the car you are selling have much open access to the back seat so that children can be strapped into their car seats with greater ease? Great. Make sure to tell them that most other cars will have them hunching down to put a child into a car seat, but with this car they can stand straight up and reach into the car with ease.

Stakes. Remember, stories are all about stakes. What pain or frustration is your product saving your customer from having to experience?

THE QUESTIONS YOU WILL WANT TO ANSWER TO STIMULATE THE RIGHT TALKING POINTS IN THIS SECTION ARE:

What negative consequence does my product help my customers avoid?

_____

_____

What will people continue to experience if they do not buy my product or service?

_____

_____

When you include the negative stakes in your marketing collateral, orders will increase.

People are driven to avoid negative consequences, so including these Soundbites in our brand narrative is going to create a sense of urgency. But we definitely don't want to leave them hanging. People are also attracted to the incredible, positive, wonderful things that will happen to them if they *do* buy our product or service.

The last element in the StoryBrand Framework will be to invite your heroic customers into a better life in which their problems are resolved.

StoryBrand Element Seven: And Experience Success

In a story, you'll want to cast a vision for your potential customer that answers the question: What's in it for me?

Every hero is looking for a "happily ever after" ending to their story, and even though the incredible benefits of buying your product may seem obvious to you, they won't be obvious to your customer.

If we want to complete the story we are inviting customers into, we need to tell them about the wonderful, powerful, positive thing that will happen to them if they buy our product or service.

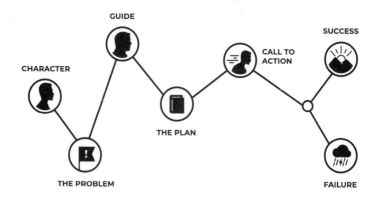

When you talk about the positive ramifications customers will experience when they use your product, you add enormous perceived economic value to your products just by using words.

For instance, in the header section of one website we show in our workshops, the small-business owner sells an electric bicycle. The bicycle costs $3,000. That's quite a hefty price for a bike. So how does she make the bike look like a great deal? She starts listing all the terrific things that happen when you buy the bike, things like:

- You will save money on gas.
- You will never have to sit in traffic.
- You get to enjoy the great outdoors.
- You get to participate in saving the environment.
- You get to be the leader of the pack.

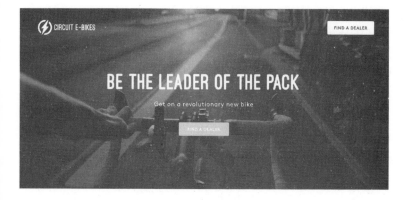

As customers read the words on your website that tell them all the value they are getting, they do some subconscious calculations. Essentially, they compare the price of the product to all the value they will be getting and the more value they get, the more appealing the price of the product.

Yes, it's true, you can change the perceived value of the products you sell using only words.

Think about it. The bike costs $3K, but you will save some of that in the cost of gas. Also, I'd pay at least $1K to never have to sit in traffic, which means the bike is actually worth $4K, but I'm only paying $3K. I'll also get to enjoy the outdoors which means I'm getting a $5K value for only $3K. But wait. I also get to save the environment. Bam! That's even more perceived value. Plus, I get to be the leader of the pack and perceived as a forward-thinking early adopter. That's huge value. At the end of the day, it feels as though this bike is worth a lot more than $3K. It might even be worth $6K or $7K because of the way it could change my life. $3,000 suddenly sounds like a great deal. And we added all that perceived value just by painting the positive stakes in our BrandScript.

Again, when you include all the wonderful things that will happen to people if they buy your product or service, you're adding perceived value to the product itself, and when you add value, people are much more likely to place an order for your product.

Painting the stakes matters. All stories are headed toward a happy or sad ending. The entire time we are watching a movie, we are hoping the hero can win the race, disarm the bomb, or get the promotion. We are hoping for these things because the storyteller has foreshadowed what the happy ending will be if the hero overcomes their challenge.

Just like in a movie, you want to continue to foreshadow what your customer's life could look like the whole time they are considering your products.

Make sure to include a list of the positive, amazing things your customer will experience if they buy your product or service. If you do, customers will start moving toward that happy ending, and they will have to buy your product or service to make that ending happen.

THE QUESTIONS YOU WANT TO ASK TO HELP CUSTOMERS IMAGINE HOW YOU CAN IMPROVE THEIR LIVES ARE:

What will my customer's life look like if they buy my product or service?

_____

_____

What benefits will my product or service provide that would add value to my customer's life?

_____

_____

When you paint a picture of the good things your customer will experience if they buy your products, you increase the perceived value of those products and your orders go up.

Now that you've given your heroic customers a vision of what their lives could look like, you've completed the process of inviting them into a story. This is a good thing. Human beings are preprogrammed to engage in stories. Their minds are always trying to organize the random data they experience every day into a narrative that makes sense. When you organize your brand message using the elements of story, your customers don't have to think as hard to understand how you can change their lives.

Now that we've got the seven categories of Soundbites down, let's talk about what to do with them so that your marketing creates as much forward thrust as possible!

Clarify Your Message by Creating a StoryBrand BrandScript

To create your seven categories of talking points, use a Story-Brand BrandScript. A BrandScript allows you to organize your thinking, clarify your message, and invite customers into an amazing story in which they use your products or services to solve their problems.

You can fill out a StoryBrand BrandScript in your Small Business Flight Plan in the back of this book.

A BrandScript looks like this:

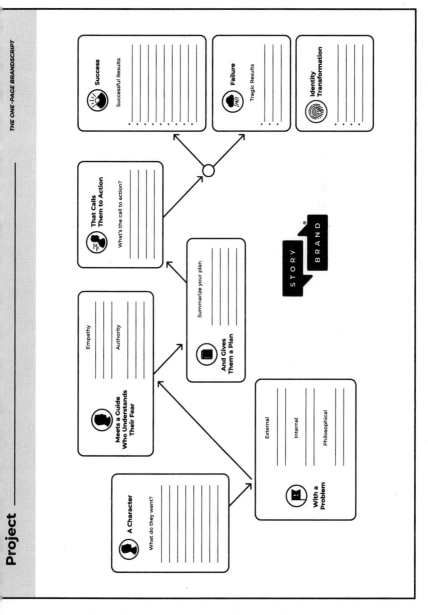

Access a digital, fillable version at SmallBusinessFlightPlan.com

Use Your New Messaging in Your Marketing Collateral

Your new marketing message can be used in all your marketing collateral, including landing pages, lead generators, emails, and even in casual conversation.

The basic principles of the StoryBrand Framework are simple:

1. Reduce your marketing to a series of repeatable Soundbites, and
2. Use those Soundbites on your landing page and your entire sales funnel.

Once you revamp your marketing collateral using your new, clear message, your customers will respond and your revenue should increase.

Now that we've fired up your right engine, let's fire up your left engine: Sales. Even if you are a solo-preneur, your plane will move through the air much faster if you learn to sell. Let's take Step Three.

Before You Read This Chapter, Accept This Challenge:

Some sales pitches work, and some don't. Who knows why? Actually, we do know why. Sales pitches that work differ, for sure. Some are funny, some are serious, some are delivered by charismatic visionaries, and some are delivered coldly by boring practitioners. What the pitches that work have in common, however, is that they invite customers (or voters or stakeholders) into a story in which the customer plays the hero and uses YOUR product to solve a problem in THEIR life. There are no exceptions. These are the pitches that work.

If you want to craft a sales pitch that closes sales (we call these "million-dollar sales pitches" because they can make any small business millions), you need to include five key elements of story and you need to do so in a very specific order.

To help you do this, we've printed this chapter in color so we can better illustrate how a pitch like this works.

Another reason we printed this chapter in color is because it may cause some readers to turn to this chapter first. That's great. If you accept the challenge to use this framework to grow your revenue, it might make you a believer in the other five frameworks that will also grow your small business.

If you own or run a small business, learning this framework may be the largest factor in getting your left engine operating with power.

If you have a sales team, make sure everybody on the team learns The Customer Is the Hero Framework and uses it in their sales conversations, follow-up emails, and proposals.

This chapter is special. If you need money for your business to stay alive, learn this framework and you will bring in more cash.

In fact, challenge yourself to send a follow-up email to every person you (or your sales team) engage in a sales conversation using the framework I'm about to introduce you to.

Follow-up emails are essential, of course, and nearly everybody sends them. But they do it wrong. What your customer needs is a crystal-clear explanation of the predicament they are in and how they can get out of it using your products. If you are clear, you will close.

Just using this framework to send out follow-up emails could significantly grow your revenue and get you the cash necessary to operate and grow your business.

Before you even read this chapter, make this commitment: you (and your sales team) will use this framework to send follow-up emails to everybody you have a sales conversation with.

Make a commitment to use The Customer Is the Hero Framework to send follow-up emails today and watch your revenue grow. Here's to your results.

3

Sales

STEP THREE:
The Left Engine

Craft a Million-Dollar Sales Pitch

Step Three Will Help You Solve These Problems:

- You hate to sell but know you need to in order to grow your business.
- You don't feel confident when you ask for the money.
- Your marketing and sales are not aligned.
- You do not know how to write a sales email that will immediately close sales.
- You keep making yourself the hero in sales conversations and it isn't working.
- Potential customers do not immediately trust you.
- Your proposals get ignored.
- You are having trouble teaching your team members how to sell.
- You need more sales and you need them now.

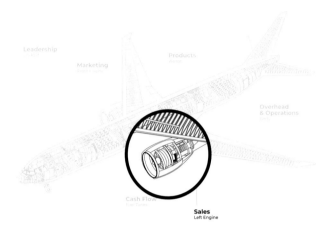

Sales
Left Engine

· · ·

Now that our right engine is generating thrust, we can use the same storytelling framework to fire up the left engine of our airplane. When you add a sales component to your plane, you double the power that pushes you through the air.

For years, we've been asked by small-business owners to apply the StoryBrand Messaging Framework to sales. This is the first time we've introduced our sales framework to business owners and leaders like yourself.

Every small-business owner and every account executive or sales rep should know how to craft a million-dollar sales pitch. What do I mean by a million-dollar sales pitch? I mean a sales pitch you can use over and over to make a million dollars, no matter how big or small your business is. If you know how to craft a great sales pitch, you can bring millions in revenue into your small business.

If you have a sales team, you will want the entire team to understand Step Three because when they understand how to craft a million-dollar sales pitch, customers will have a more positive interaction with your brand and sales will increase.

In fact, at the end of this step I will challenge you to use the framework to write a sales letter that will more than pay for the money and time you've invested in this book.

Very few of us who run or own a small business think of ourselves as salespeople, but the truth is, we all have to sell. If we don't tell others about our products in such a way they understand how we can solve their problems, our small businesses will crash.

If you don't like to sell, don't worry. *The Customer Is the Hero Sales Framework* will teach you to stop thinking about selling and instead craft a pitch that invites customers into a story.

If you hate to sell, I understand, but if this is true about you let's take a moment to change the way we think of sales. Instead of trying to trick or manipulate people into buying our product, let's simply explain how our product will solve their problems and allow the customer to decide whether or not they want to buy it.

The big rub when we encounter salespeople is that we feel they're not being honest about something. The interaction can make us feel that the salesperson we are talking to just wants our money. The relationship feels transactional and inauthentic, which bothers us.

Several years ago, for example, my wife and I went down to a local car dealership to buy her a car. We were there for hours, going through their inventory, test-driving cars, and finally haggling about price. The process took so long I actually left and brought back dinner for the three of us: my wife, myself, and the sales guy. I was fine with that, though, because at the end of the process, the salesperson gave us $10,000 off on the car we wanted. He had to check with his manager five times and really crunch the numbers, but we got the deal done. I couldn't have been happier until my wife and I got home and sat down on the couch to turn off our brains and watch television. No kidding, one of the first commercials that came on was from that car dealership. The commercial obnoxiously proclaimed that anybody who walked in the door would get $10,000 off a new car!

I felt used, manipulated, and foolish. My wife just giggled. "It was nice of you to buy him dinner," she said, patting me on the knee.

So how do we keep from making people feel used or manipulated? Easy. Don't use or manipulate people.

Instead of selling somebody something, let's invite them into an honest story in which they are able to solve a problem by using the products we sell.

Whenever I'm in a sales conversation, I don't give a second's effort to trying to convince the customer to buy anything. Instead, all my energy is focused on a single question: *Does this customer have a problem my product can solve?* If they do, I tell them about my products. If they don't, I don't sell them anything.

In fact, there have been many times when a potential customer has wanted to buy my product, but I talked them out of it. I honestly didn't believe my product would work for them, and as a small-business owner, I can't afford to have a single customer dissatisfied with my product. Dissatisfied customers will crash your airplane fast. Take my word for it: Do anything you can to keep from selling products to people who don't need them.

There's a benefit to this commitment. When we stop thinking about trying to convince people they need something and instead try to find out if they have a problem our products can solve, both the sales conversation and the satisfaction of the customer after they buy the product (along with the word-of-mouth that spreads about you and your products) all go up. This amounts to a million-dollar sales pitch. And more.

The truth is it's possible for people to explain what they offer, solve their customers' problems, and grow their companies without coming off as sleazy.

In order to do that, though, here's the big paradigm shift we need to understand: Instead of engaging in exhausting and manipulative sales conversations in which we try to convince people to buy something, let's make the customer the hero and invite them into a story in which we help them solve a problem.

As you know, we've already done this with our marketing. The StoryBrand Framework helped you come up with fixed Soundbites you can use to populate marketing collateral. That part, though, is easy. You just come up with Soundbites, stick them on websites and in automated emails, and let them rest for years.

Sales, though, is dynamic. Sales conversations happen over lunch, in text message exchanges, and over Zoom calls. With *The Customer Is the Hero Sales Framework*, we are going to learn to actually think in story.

The greatest business leaders, political leaders, and religious leaders have all been exceptional salespeople. In fact, I firmly believe that Richard Branson, Mother Teresa, Oprah Winfrey, Mahatma Gandhi, Winston Churchill, and nearly any other leader you admire knows *The Customer Is the Hero Sales Framework* intuitively. And the more you use it, the more influence, impact, and sales success you can have. Were they trying to sell? No. They were trying to solve people's problems.

So how do we do this effortlessly and naturally? We use a color-coded system that teaches us how to guide a conversation so it's helpful to every customer we encounter.

The Customer Is the Hero: The Sales Framework for People Who Need to Sell

When we're sitting across from a customer having a conversation or when we're responding to an email inquiry, how do we "think in story?"

The key to all good sales conversations is understanding the story is not about us. We don't need to spend a single second trying to convince people how great we are. Regardless of whether we're having lunch with a potential client, checking in on the phone, or following up via email, we want to keep in mind that our customer is a hero in a story, and they are actively trying to solve a problem. If we have them and their story in mind each time we speak or communicate through email, we will best be able to guide them toward a purchase that will in turn solve their problem and resolve their story.

This means we should be much more interested in finding out if the person we are interacting with has a problem we can solve than we are in convincing them to buy a product they may not need.

When you "think in story" your conversations are much more interesting to potential customers, no matter the size of your business.

After learning to make the customer the hero, Steve Rusing, Senior VP of US Sales at Tempur Sealy International, the largest mattress company in the world, said that he and his team stopped "selling" their products to retail partners and, instead, met with them to inquire about the goals of their individual stores. Once they understood what their retail partners wanted to accomplish, they helped them position Tempur Sealy products to meet those goals.

Steve told me their retail partners had never had a mattress company ask them what their goals were or what they were trying to do with their stores. Sadly, mattress stores were more accustomed to mattress companies "using them" to accomplish their sales goals rather than working with the retailer to understand and accomplish their own goals. When Tempur Sealy found out what the hero wanted and came up with a campaign to help them reach their goals, everybody's sales went up.

When business owners understand that the customer is the hero and treat them as such, they sell more product. And they do so without selling. All of this might sound complicated, but it isn't. To think in story, all you need to do is think in color.

Here's what I mean.

A long time ago a broadband business called and asked if I could consult with their sales team. They were struggling to close deals because they kept getting into the weeds describing all the technical capabilities of their products. Customers often looked at them blank-eyed, as though they'd been presented a complicated math riddle rather than a solution to their problem. To help make the customer the hero, they asked if I would review some of their sales collateral.

The first piece they wanted me to look at was a two-page proposal that, if accepted, would result in a sale worth millions. The proposal seemed good and clear but it was missing something. It was missing a story. The proposal clearly explained what would be included in the package of products they believed the customer needed, but the proposal read flat. It just wasn't interesting.

I explained to the sales team how a sales pitch that invites a customer into a story works, that a story is almost always about a hero who overcomes a problem to experience a better life. We were meeting on Zoom, so I shared my screen and started using different highlight colors to deconstruct the proposal.

"Any text that describes the customer's problem I'm going to highlight in red," I said. "Any text that talks about the life they're going to be able to experience if they buy your product, I'll highlight in blue," I continued. "The parts where you talk about your products, I'll highlight in purple."

"Got it," they said. Then I started reading the document out loud, highlighting as I went. They were amazed when I was done. The document was covered in one color: purple.

All they'd done in the proposal was talk about themselves and their products without framing their products as the tools the customer could use to solve their problems and live happily ever after. This is the opposite of a million-dollar sales pitch.

Fixing the proposal so it honored the customer as the hero was easy. We simply wrote a few sentences at the beginning of the proposal that identified the customer's problem (red) and then added a few sentences at the end of the proposal that identified what the customer's life would look like if they said yes to the proposal (blue).

After we color-coded the proposal, we could clearly see that we'd invited the customer into a story. The proposal started out with some red, flowed into some purple, and ended up with a splash of blue. In other words: The proposal identified the customer's problem, described their product as the solution to that problem, and painted a picture of the better life that was possible once the customer's problem was resolved. Suddenly we had a million-dollar sales pitch.

The sales team closed the deal in large part because they made the customer the hero and invited them into a story.

That consulting conversation was so helpful, I created a color key that will allow any of us to have great sales conversations, write great emails, and create better proposals. It even teaches us to "think in story" when we're in casual conversation.

Since that meeting with the broadband company, I've added a few more story elements and color-coded them so you will be able to see, at a glance, whether or not you are inviting the customer into a solid story. The color key is similar to the Story-Brand Marketing Framework but because the sales framework needs to be active and fluid, I simplified it.

The best way to think of *The Customer Is the Hero Sales Framework* is that it's like chords on a guitar. Each color is a different chord you can use to create any number of songs you want. Once you know the chords, you can create art. As long as you've got a few colors represented in whatever document you are writing or conversation you are having, the customer will hear the music and clearly be able to identify the story you are inviting them into.

In fact, if you want to sell more of your products, take each one (or at least your top sellers) and create a sales letter using the color-coded *The Customer Is the Hero Sales Framework*. But don't stop at just a sales letter. Use those same talking points in your sales conversations, presentations, and elevator pitch. *The Customer Is the Hero Sales Framework* will be your secret weapon to close more sales.

Any small-business leader who "thinks in story" will have the equivalent of a jet engine strapped to the left wing of their business. If your sales team can "think in story" your plane is going to move forward with a great deal more thrust. There is no question sales will increase.

The "The Customer Is the Hero" color key looks like this:

The customer's problem: red

Your product positioned as the solution: purple

The three- or four-step plan: brown

The negative consequence you are saving the customer from: yellow

The positive result your customer will experience: blue

Your call to action: green

If you can include two or more colors in a customer interaction (an email, proposal, a conversation over lunch) then you're inviting a customer into a story and they're going to be much more likely to pay attention. If you can include three or four, all the better. If you can include all six then you have just crafted a million-dollar sales pitch without even thinking about selling.

The key is for all of this to become so natural you think in story intuitively.

What Does It Look Like to Invite a Customer into a Story?

Let's say you're at a cocktail party, and you meet two people who do the exact same job. They have the same type of small business that offers the same service with the same quality and the same price.

You're talking with the first person and ask them what they do. They answer, "I'm an at-home chef. I come to your house and cook."

You'd likely find this person interesting and begin asking how they got into a career in cooking. You might want to know where they went to school or what their favorite restaurants in town happen to be. You'd make casual conversation and probably enjoy the interaction, but you'd be unlikely to get their number and inquire about whether or not they could cook for you. In fact, it would never occur to you that an at-home chef might be exactly what you and your family need.

Later, while talking to the second person about what they do, you notice they answer differently. They say, "You know how most families don't eat together anymore? And when they do, they don't eat healthy. I'm an at-home chef. I come to your house and cook so you and your family can actually connect with each other over a great meal and when you're done, you don't have to worry about cleaning up."

Now *that's* a completely different way of answering the question! *That's* a chef you might consider hiring because they invited you into a story.

What's the story? The story is about you, the hero parent who hired an at-home chef so you could better connect with your family over dinner. And when you hear that story, you're much more likely to want to actually live it. What do you need to do to live that story? You need to hire this person to be your at-home chef.

How Do You Use "The Customer Is the Hero" Color Key to Sell?

Let's break down The Customer Is the Hero color key to analyze how this storytelling methodology works.

Identify the Customer's Problem—Red

If you were only going to include one color in your conversation, you'd want to include the color red. Red text represents the problem your customer is having and will do more to engage a potential customer than any other color.

The problem is the "hook" in the story. Until our hero encounters a problem, we don't pay much attention, which is why, when you're watching a movie, the hero gets into trouble quickly. When a storyteller introduces the hero's problem, a "story loop" opens up in the audience's mind: Will the hero be able to solve this problem?

The same is true when we start talking about our customer's problem in a sales conversation. When we identify their problem, a story loop opens in their mind and, of course, the only thing that will close the story loop (resolve the problem) is our product or service. In other words: They're hooked.

When we mention the problem our customer has, our customer thinks: Do you have a solution? Will your solution work for me?

Why is the problem so important when we're having a sales conversation?

Human beings are problem-solving machines. We are hard-wired to engage challenges and overcome them. Even as I watch my ten-month-old daughter learn to lift a spoon and rub baby food on her head, I'm watching a lifelong problem-solver get started on her path to solve (and conquer) the million fun and exciting problems set before her.

In fact, human beings love to solve problems so ferociously that if they don't have any problems, they will invent them. Ever been around somebody who likes to stir up drama? Why do they do that? They want a problem to talk about and have an opinion about and tinker with.

Again, as humans, we absolutely love to think about problems and then solve them.

For this reason, it's only when we associate our product as a solution to our customer's problem that they begin to think about making a purchase. Until your potential customer connects your product to their problem, they will not think much about your product at all. Therefore, the most important thing you can do in sales is talk about your customer's problem. When you do, they lean in to learn more.

Let's look at what our successful new chef friend said using the "The Customer Is the Hero" story-based color-code.

"You know how most families don't eat together anymore and when they do, they don't eat healthy . . ."

Bam! Right out of the gate, our chef opens a story loop. And he does more than that. He's actually qualifying the customer. By saying, "You know how most families don't eat together anymore . . ." he's finding out if the person he's talking to has the problem his product resolves. If they do, they're already leaning in to hear the rest of the sentence; if they don't, he can just enjoy a casual conversation and move on. In sales, your main objective is to find out whether the person you are talking to has the problem that your product solves. No strong-arming. No manipulation. No sleazy, coercive conversation.

The point is this: Start every sales conversation by identifying your customer's problem.

Position Your Product as the Solution—Purple

A powerful thing happens when you position your product as the solution to a problem: The perceived value of your product skyrockets.

In life we attribute value to one thing and one thing only: solutions. A heart surgeon is the solution to a potentially fatal problem, so we value heart surgeons a great deal. A safe family car is a solution to any anxiety we might feel about carrying our kids around in a dangerous vehicle. A Rolex watch is the solution to a desire for status.

If we're honest, we even see the people we love as solutions to a problem. My wife is a solution to my loneliness and my desire for romance, family, and adventure. I value her a great deal because she's a wonderful solution to what could have easily been a big problem in my life. Even our children are solutions to our heart's desire for meaning and our inherent need to sacrifice for and enjoy another.

The point is this: In a sales conversation, talk about your product as the solution to a problem and the people you're talking to will place greater value on the product itself.

In fact, whenever I start to read a nonfiction book, my mind races to answer one question: What problem is this book going to help me solve? If I can't answer that question within a few pages, my mind wanders, and the book inevitably ends up in the large pile of unread books on my nightstand.

It's simple: We value people and things that solve problems.

Here's another truth: The perceived value of a product increases or decreases based on the severity of the problem it resolves. The more serious the problem, the greater value we place on its solution. Clearly articulating how our product solves a problem is important to the perceived worth of that product.

Let's look again at our chef's answer to the question "What do you do?" to see how he includes his service as the solution to a problem:

> "You know how most families don't eat together anymore?
> And when they do, they don't eat healthy. I'm an at-home chef.
> I come to your house and cook . . ."

When the chef opens with the problem his customer may have and then immediately positions his product as the solution, the listener determines that his service is valuable. He also opens and closes a story loop:

> "What do we do if we don't eat together anymore as a family?
> We hire this chef to come to our home and cook."

In a way, when we opened our story loop by stating the problem and then offered to close it by positioning our product or service as the solution to the problem, we invited our customer into a story. Remember, a story is always about a hero who wants something and has to overcome conflict to get it. A story about how their family can overcome the challenge of not eating together anymore by hiring an at-home chef is a great story to invite a customer into if (and only if) our potential customer has the problem we have described.

If we simply take the first two steps in *The Customer Is the Hero Sales Framework*, we will close more sales. It's true, if you just have a red sentence or two and a purple sentence or two in your sales email, proposal, presentation, or even as talking points in casual conversations, you will close more sales. Many more sales. But we're not done. There is still another color we can add to further invite customers into a story.

Give Your Customer a Plan—Brown

At this point in the story you're inviting customers into, they know you have a solution to their problem. Often, though, this isn't enough information to cause them to place an order.

As we discussed while talking about the StoryBrand Marketing Framework, the reason your customer is unlikely to place an order is because placing an order requires them to take a risk. They could lose their money. They could feel like a fool. They could find out the product or service doesn't fit their needs like they thought it would. In short, placing an order involves changing their lives in some way, and most people resist change.

Let's look a little closer at the moment of pause and concern a customer experiences in the buying journey. When a customer realizes you have a solution to their problem, they have to make a decision about whether or not to buy that solution, so, at this point, they might experience a bit of cognitive dissonance. This cognitive dissonance is going to feel like confusion or perhaps concern, but they won't know exactly why.

Imagine the customer journey as a hike through the woods. At this point in the journey, the trail they are on suddenly descends into a rushing river. By giving the customer a plan, you effectively build a bridge from the customer's problem to your solution. Again, this bridge can be built by including a three-step plan the customer can follow to buy your product and solve their problem.

For example: If our chef friend included a three-step plan in the story he invites customers into, it might go something like this:

"You know how most families don't eat together anymore? And when they do, they don't eat healthy. I'm an at-home chef. I come to your house and cook.

"If you ever want to try it, the process is simple. We have a quick thirty-minute meeting in which I find out what your family likes to eat, what food allergies exist, and so on. Then I come to your house and make dinner. That costs about $100. Then, if you want to make that a regular thing, we figure out when you'd like to fit me in with your family's schedule."

Did you catch the chef's three-step plan? First, he has an intake meeting. Second, he comes over and cooks a meal. Third, he enters into a retainer agreement.

When we offer a three-step plan, our customer is much more likely to cross the bridge from their problem to our solution.

When the chef gave his customer a step-by-step plan, he did two things:

First, he reduced the sense of risk. The customer would likely have been interested in the service based on what the chef had already explained, but the customer would likely not have moved forward because of too many unknowns. How often would the chef be there? Would it feel awkward for him to take over the kitchen? Would the chef be able to cook around the family's food allergies? How much would all this cost, and what if the family didn't like the food?

When the chef rolled out his simple plan, he mitigated the customer's risk by reducing the process into a series of baby steps.

The second thing the chef did when he included the three-step plan was give the customer a clear picture of what the future would look like. Human beings don't like change, even positive change, because change involves risk. What if, after hiring him, life got worse, not better? When the chef foreshadowed the customer's future, he replaced fear with a hopeful vision of the future.

Think about it. Let's say you're selling mattresses. You know the customer you're talking to has back issues, and you know their old mattress is making their back problems worse. Yet they won't place an order. Why not? There are likely a few reasons. First, what if the mattress makes their back feel even worse? Second, what are they going to do with their old mattress? Third, what if the new mattress is great but softens quickly and loses its firmness? Maybe the new mattress isn't worth it. Who knows? It's an expensive risk to take.

If our mattress sales representative offers a three-step plan, though, they can alleviate all those fears. They simply need to say: First, we deliver the mattress to your house. Second, we take away your old mattress. Third, we stick by our product. If in ninety days you don't like your mattress, we will take it back and apply your investment to any other mattress in the showroom.

The point is this: When you build a bridge from your customer's problem to your solution, you alleviate risk, make the transition process clear, and increase the chances your customer will cross over and place an order.

Just remember this when it comes to spelling out the three- or four-step plan: Explain how easy the transition is from not using your product and having a problem, to using your product and solving said problem.

Don't let your customer stand at the edge of the river fearfully watching the water flow by. Build a bridge by giving them a plan.

Now that we've started with the problem, positioned our product as the solution, and built a bridge from the customer's problem to our solution, it's time to create a sense of urgency.

Paint the Stakes and Create a Sense of Urgency— Yellow and *Blue*

There's nothing better at the end of a movie than a happy ending. When the couple gets married or the bad guy is caught or the lawyer wins the case, we cheer. I can still remember standing on my seat as a kid as Daniel won the karate tournament in *The Karate Kid*. Why? Because I'd spent the previous hour biting my nails at the threat of Daniel being beaten up by the bully and humiliated in front of the girl he liked! In other words, the storytellers gave me a bunch of really good reasons to care.

The same factor that drives engagement in a movie can drive engagement in the story you are inviting customers into.

To increase engagement in a story, storytellers paint the stakes by constantly reminding the audience what could be won or lost if the hero does or does not accomplish the task at hand.

If you watch movies closely, you'll notice the screenwriters will foreshadow a climactic scene. Sometimes this scene is called the "obligatory scene" because the storyteller is obligated to show it to us. My family and I were watching *National Treasure 2* the other day. About fifteen minutes into the movie, Justin Bartha's character turns to Nicolas Cage and says, "They're going to try to steal the Declaration of Independence" to which Nicolas Cage says in a gritty tone, "And we're going to stop them."

There you go. A scene in which Nicolas Cage tries to stop the bad guys from stealing the Declaration of Independence is now the obligatory scene.

In fact, it's often true that a screenwriter will write the obligatory scene and then go back and write the movie so that the obligatory scene is as emotionally fulfilling as possible. A good screenplay will often be reverse engineered with the ending in mind.

The same goes for sales: You'll want to foreshadow an obligatory scene your customer can move toward.

For instance: If you're a real estate agent and want to sell a house, simply find out what the homeowner hates most about their current home and foreshadow an obligatory scene that involves the resolution of that problem. Does your client hate the fact that the master bathroom only has one sink? Great. Remind them how it's way too difficult for her and her husband to get ready in the morning with only one sink. Let her know you're going to get her into a house that has a large, spacious bathroom and *two sinks!*

Did you see what the real estate agent did there? They fore-shadowed a climactic scene in which the home buyer stood in a spacious bathroom with two sinks. That sort of vision casting gives the buyer a sense of urgency to close the story loop in their mind and buy the new, better house.

Remember, the obligatory scene is always, always the scene in which the primary problem in the story is resolved. So, if you listen well and understand the problem your customer is hoping to resolve and then foreshadow an obligatory scene in which their problem is resolved using your product or service, the energy in the story they are being invited into will run toward that obligatory resolution.

How Does Foreshadowing a Climactic Scene Increase Customer Engagement?

When you foreshadow a climactic or obligatory scene, you create something called cognitive dissonance, and cognitive dissonance is how stories generate narrative traction. Essentially, cognitive dissonance is a tension that builds and builds until it's released by the resolution of the problem. Cognitive dissonance isn't always uncomfortable—it can often be fun and entertaining. For crying out loud, will the team win the championship or not?!

For our real estate agent friend, foreshadowing the climactic scene creates a little cognitive dissonance that only a master bathroom with two sinks will resolve.

As the agent walks through each of the houses that she shows a client, she can foreshadow what the reality of living in this house would be like: Nancy would have plenty of room in the bathroom; Jim would have a fence around the backyard and would never have to wander the neighborhood in the middle of the night looking for the dog; the baby could be checked on without climbing any stairs. Perfect. That's three climactic scenes the agent has foreshadowed, thus channeling the energy toward the resolution of three different problems in the customer's story.

Every time the agent brings up a climactic scene, the customer feels two things. First, they feel listened to. Rather than talking endlessly about mortgage rates and cabinet space and the new water heater—three things the customer never mentioned—the agent has listened to and understood the story of her customers and is guiding them in the direction they want to go. Second, the customer feels a clear and actionable way to find closure in the story of finding a home.

Add Negative Stakes to Increase the Urgency Even More

Positive stakes aren't the only tool you can use to increase urgency in a story. When you add negative stakes to the talking points of your sales conversations, sales go up even more.

Will Nancy have to continue to bump into her husband in their small master bath? Will Jim have to continue to roam the neighborhood looking for the dog all the time? What negative experiences will your customers have or continue to have if they do not buy your product?

When we paint a picture of the success our customer will experience, along with the frustrations our product or service will keep them from experiencing, customers are much more likely to place an order. Let's add some positive and negative stakes to the dialogue our friend the chef is having at the cocktail party:

"You know how most families don't eat together anymore? And when they do, they don't eat healthy. I'm an at-home chef. I come to your house and cook.

"If you ever want to try it, the process is simple. We have a quick thirty-minute meeting in which I find out what your family likes to eat, what food allergies exist, and so on. Then I come to your house and make dinner. That costs about $100. Then, if you want to make that a regular thing, we figure out when you'd like to fit me in with your family's schedule.

"There are only so many family dinners left before the kids go off on their own.

"My clients sit comfortably at dinner and actually engage with each other. Day after day, they get to know each other a little better and feel supported, listened to, and cared for. All because, at least for a couple days each week, they don't have to cook!"

Do you see how adding positive and negative stakes creates a sense of urgency?

Adding stakes to your sales conversations makes the story you are inviting customers into more interesting.

Now let's add the final talking point and start closing some sales.

Call Your Customer to Action—Green

The reason top salespeople got to be top salespeople is because they were good at asking for the order. Jerry Jones, owner of the Dallas Cowboys, once said there are three rules in business: The first is to always ask for the money and he couldn't remember the other two.

If you get good at calling your customer to action, your small business is going to grow.

Still, most small-business owners hate asking for the money. It makes them feel sleazy and pushy. But let's change the way we view that exchange. After all, what is really happening when we ask for the sale?

If you really knew what was happening in your customer's mind after you invited them into a story, you'd ask for the sale every time. Here's what I mean:

A few years ago my wife and I had a long wait in an overseas airport, so we decided to walk around and look in some of the shops in the terminal. This was a big airport with what amounted to a shopping mall in the middle. As I walked around the mall, I found myself perusing a jewelry counter that contained watches. For at least two years I'd been wanting to buy a nice watch. A few years earlier I'd scaled my company past a certain revenue mark. I'd told myself that when I did so, I'd get myself a little reward, something to wear on my wrist that I could pass down to my children when they got older. Two years had passed, though, and I hadn't bought the watch. I'd bought more than a few nice watches for friends and team members, but it always seemed too luxurious to buy something like that for myself. My wife kept bothering me to buy the watch, but it never felt right.

The salesperson came up and asked if I wanted to try anything on. I told him I did and pointed at a nice, entry-level dress watch. When he asked why I was interested in that particular watch, I told him I'd scaled my company past my goal, and I'd been putting off getting myself a reward for a couple years. He smiled and said I certainly deserved it. I thanked him but ultimately took the watch off and told him I'd continue to think about it.

"You don't want to buy this watch," he said, forthrightly.

"Not today," I reluctantly responded.

Then he did something I thought was really special, something for which I'm grateful.

"Don, would you like for me to box this watch up so you can take it home and keep it as a token of your accomplishment?" he asked with a smile, an expression on his face that said, *Help me help you.*

I paused for a moment to consider his question, then said, "Yes. That's exactly what I want you to do."

When I got back to my wife and showed her the watch, she was shocked.

"You actually did it!" she exclaimed. "It's beautiful. What made you buy this one?"

I told her I didn't know. At the time it was true; I really didn't know what made me pull the trigger. Now I know I chose that watch because the salesperson gave me permission to do what I already wanted to do: He gave me permission to treat myself.

And you know what? I love that watch. I'll give that watch to one of my kids or to a friend someday, and I'll tell them about how hard it is to build a company but how, if you keep going and continue to offer value, your dreams can come true.

I can't tell you how grateful I am that a salesman in the airport was professional and confident enough to call me to action. I really did want the watch. I had the money. I just needed a little help.

Sometimes Your Customer Just Wants You to Give Them Permission to Do What They Already Want to Do—Place an Order

Chances are you don't consider yourself a professional salesperson, but if you run or own a small business, learning to call your customers to action can significantly increase your revenue.

The guy at the watch counter was not manipulating me. He knew I could afford the watch because I'd told him I'd grown my company, and he also knew I wanted the watch for a good reason. What he did when he called me to action was give me a little confidence that I was making a good decision. He was just letting me know I wouldn't regret buying the watch, and he was right—I have no regrets at all.

Most small-business leaders fear being pushy or overbearing with their customers, so they don't use clear calls to action in their sales conversations. Because of that, though, their sales interactions sound passive and weak, like this:

"It was great talking to you. If you ever need my help or want to talk more, let me know."

This is what the customer hears when they encounter such a weak call to action:

"I don't believe my product will solve your problem, but I want you to like me anyway. If you ever want to give me some charity in exchange for this product, which again, will probably not meet your needs, please do so because I have a mortgage to pay and kids to feed."

This call to action lacks confidence.

When I talk about confidence, I'm not talking about being confident in yourself. I certainly hope you are confident in yourself as a person, but you don't have to be confident in yourself as a person to be good at sales. In sales, you only have to be confident about one thing: that your product will solve your customer's problem.

If you aren't sure your product can solve your customer's problem, stop now and improve your product. Keep working at it until it works better than anything else on the market (for that price), and soon you'll have all the confidence you need to sell it.

People who represent quality don't apologize for their offering. They know what their product or service is worth.

If you know your product or service will solve your customers' problems, call them to action with confidence.

Make Your Calls to Action Clear

Another mistake small-business leaders make when it comes to calling their customers to action is they fail to make the call to action clear. Statements like: "Would you like to learn more?" or "Would you be interested in trying this out?" are actually not clear calls to action. Clear calls to action tell the customer exactly what they need to do to either buy the product or start the process of buying the product or service.

Statements such as: "Can I box this up for you?" or "We can be there on Thursday to install the machine. Do you want to buy it today?" are not statements the customer will be confused about. A good call to action does not give the customer a *path to consider*, it gives the customer *a purchasing decision to accept or reject*.

Again, our friend, the chef:

"You know how most families don't eat together anymore? And when they do, they don't eat healthy. I'm an at-home chef. I come to your house and cook.

"If you ever want to try it, the process is simple. We have a quick thirty-minute meeting in which I find out what your family likes to eat, what food allergies exist, and so on. Then I come to your house and make dinner. That costs about $100. Then, if you want to make that a regular thing, we figure out when you'd like to fit me in with your family's schedule.

"There are only so many family dinners left before the kids go off on their own.

"My clients sit comfortably at dinner and actually engage with each other. Day after day, they get to know each other a little better and feel supported, listened to, and cared for. All because, at least for a couple days each week, they don't have to cook!

"I have time next Thursday to meet about cooking for your family. Would you like to get together?"

Once our chef friend gives the customer a purchasing decision to accept or reject, the customer knows exactly what they need to do to solve their problem and can make a decision to step into the story or go a different way.

Rejection Isn't the End of the World

Naturally, if you give customers something to accept or reject, you're going to get more rejections than you used to get before you included a strong call to action. This is an unfortunate fact. Many people are not going to be ready to make a purchase no matter what you do, and this may lead to an uncomfortable exchange in which they reject your offer.

This is easy enough to resolve, though. If our chef is rejected, they simply need to say something like, "If you know anybody who could use a home chef, let me know. I've got room for two more families. Enough about me. What do you do?"

From this point on, you have made the story you invite people into perfectly clear and there's no need to sell any further. The key to sales is clarity, not pushiness. By changing the subject and getting to know the person you are talking to a little bit, you ease all the discomfort of the rejection. The key to accepting rejection without making it feel awkward is for you, the person who is making the sale, to set the customer at ease for deciding not to move forward. When the person you're talking to senses you are not the least bit uncomfortable having been rejected, they won't be the least bit uncomfortable either. In fact, they will respect you more because, unlike most people, you are not afraid to ask for something you want. Rejection is part of life, and, honestly, it's of no concern to most successful people. The customer isn't rejecting *you*, after all—they're just saying they don't have the problem you are able to fix. Great. If they ever do have that problem, now they know who to call. And what's more, if they have a friend who has that problem, they can refer them to you.

The good news about including a strong call to action in your talking points is that even though you are going to get rejected more than you did before, you are also going to make more sales than you ever have before. Because you made the call to action clear, more people are going to decide to buy your product and your left engine is going to create more thrust. In fact, you'll find that when you make your call to action clear, your sales will increase dramatically.

One of the main differences between successful and unsuccessful small-business owners selling a good product is that successful business owners make their calls to action as clear as possible.

Memorize Your Call to Action

Clear calls to action aren't going to come naturally. We all get a little timid when it's time to ask for the sale.

After you learn the color-coded *The Customer Is the Hero Sales Framework*, you will start to invite customers into a story intuitively. But there's only one part of the framework in which I'd recommend memorizing a "line" you can use over and over: the call to action.

It's scary to ask people to make a purchase. However, if you memorize your call to action and say it as a predetermined line, you'll find it works, and the more it works, the more natural it will feel to say it.

My guess is the guy at the jewelry store in the airport had said, "Would you like for me to box this up so you can take it with you on the plane" to thousands of people, many of whom, like me, answered with a "yes." And once again, I am grateful he had that line prepared because I like that watch and I'm glad I own it.

The call to action you memorize could go something like this:

"My team can mow your lawn this Saturday and handle your landscaping every week from here on out. Want my team to show up at your place on Saturday? I can just leave an invoice in your mailbox."

Any landscaper who uses that line every time they invite customers into a story is going to ramp up their left engine and grow their business. Fast.

If you have a product you believe in, have confidence in that product and call your customers to action.

When you learn to make the customer the hero using the six colors I've introduced you to in this chapter, you can easily craft million-dollar sales pitches intuitively, and without thinking about selling. With this "sales pitch" our chef could easily book millions in cooking and catering business over the span of a few short years and, if they branched out to other cities and hired more chefs to be on their team, millions and millions more. The framework isn't about coercion and it's hardly even about sales; it's about clarity. Again, when customers understand how your product can solve their problem, they place orders.

Ramp Up Your Left Engine by Making the Customer the Hero

Years ago when my business was much smaller, I debated hiring a full-time sales representative. We'd grown our business through our sales funnel and were having no problem finding and serving customers. Hiring a sales representative, thus, seemed like an unnecessary risk.

After thinking about it, though, I realized that sales representatives are usually paid a small base salary and earn the rest of their income through commissions. If you're building an airplane, this is great because it means your overhead (in this case, salary expenditure) increases minimally and only expands if the salesperson sells enough to generate commissions. So I decided to hire a sales representative.

That proved to be one of the best decisions I ever made. My new sales representative made the customer the hero and closed the same amount of sales my marketing funnel was able to create and close, which nearly doubled our revenue.

These days we have a small sales team that continues to account for over 50 percent of our sales. Both our right and left engines are ripping through the sky and, not only this, but because we are getting constant feedback from our sales team about what our clients want, we've been able to create new products that add to the strength and size of the wings.

If you have a product customers love and are considering hiring a sales representative, I'd advise you to do so. Just make sure they know how to make the customer the hero, and the left engine of your airplane should help you fly farther and faster.

Not quite ready to hire a sales rep? I understand. But here's a little challenge that will help you more fully believe in *The Customer Is the Hero Sales Framework*: Use the framework to write a sales letter that generates thousands of dollars in business.

You've got a sample of the framework in your Small Business Flight Plan (and there's a free digital version at OnlineSales Script.com) that will allow you to create the perfect talking points you can use in a sales email. Is there a sale you've had trouble closing? Is there a product you can write a sales letter about and send that letter to your email list?

I challenge you to sit down and use the framework to write a sales letter, close a few sales, and put thousands of dollars in your operating account. When you do, you will realize how simple it is to ramp up your right engine and get your business growing again.

With that, let's take a look at what these right and left engines are actually selling. Let's optimize your product offering so your airplane gets even greater (and easier) lift. Let's look at the wings of your airplane.

If you are struggling to craft good sales pitches, our design team created a digital tool at SmallBusinessFlightPlan.com that will color code your sales pitch for you. I use it all the time to help clients craft great sales pitches. Feel free to play with it yourself. It's super helpful.

Products

STEP FOUR:
The Wings

Optimize Your Product Offering with the Product Optimization Playbook

Step Four Will Help You Solve These Problems:

- You aren't sure which of your products is really producing the most profit.
- You could use a new product that increases your profitability.
- Your product offering is getting boring to your customers.
- You have wasted many hours launching a product that didn't sell.
- You need more cash and you need it fast.
- You do not have a process in place to upsell products to existing customers.

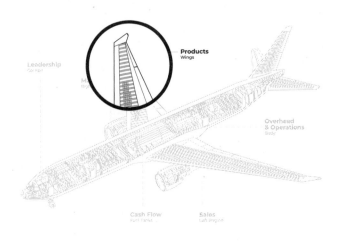

- - -

What gives your airplane lift? The wings. The right and left engines, as powerful as they may be, will not contribute to lift without a strong set of wings. Your marketing and sales engines only work if they have product to sell. And what that product is, how it came to be, whether or not it is bundled with other products, and how profitable those products are all contribute to the success or failure of your small business.

The same is true of the products you sell through your small business. Your business gets off the ground only when your marketing and sales engines move product. The kinds of products we choose to create and sell, then, matter as much to the flight of our business as the wings matter to an airplane. If the products are not in demand and profitable, it will be as though the wings of our airplane are too small. Could an airplane like that work? For sure. But only if the marketing and sales engines are strong enough to overcome the lack of surface area that would otherwise create lift.

When you optimize your product offering for demand and profitability and prioritize products that create more lift, it's as though you are enlarging and strengthening the wings of your aircraft, allowing it to take flight with greater ease.

If you had to increase your current revenue by 25 percent in six months, what would your first move be? Likely, you'd ramp up your marketing and sales engines. That makes sense. If the right and left engines gain more power, the plane will fly faster. What if, though, I removed those options? What if you had to increase your revenue by 25 percent and weren't allowed to touch your marketing or sales engines? If that were the case, you'd only have one option, an option that most small-business owners forget they have: to optimize your product offering.

When we think about growing our business, we rarely think about optimizing our product offerings. This is a mistake. There are thousands, if not millions, of dollars to be made by optimizing the products you sell for greater demand and profitability.

On my podcast, I recently spoke with two women who own a dance studio in Salt Lake City. As we discussed increasing their revenue, they mentioned they wanted to franchise and build another location. What do you think I heard when they said that? I heard, "Let's bloat the body of the airplane!" Sure, they could increase revenue that way, but another location would create a tremendous amount of additional overhead.

When I asked them what their top revenue-generating products were, they told me the first was beginner dance lessons for little kids, followed by break dancing (soon to be an Olympic sport, apparently), and a few other classes.

"How much do you charge to teach people how to break dance?" I asked.

"About $250 for six classes."

"That's six weeks' worth of classes you have to teach, right?"

"Yes," they said, "our instructor teaches six 90 minute classes."

After they told me what the instructor got paid and how many people signed up for each class, I realized they weren't making much profit. Still, the only way they figured they could scale was to open another location and duplicate their current model.

That's the way most small-business owners think. It's not a terrible way to think but it's not the best way, either.

The real question we all want to ask when it comes to optimizing our product offering is this: How can I work just as hard as I'm working now and generate two, five, or even ten times the revenue?

Sound crazy? It isn't crazy at all. All you have to do is figure out how to work just as hard as you're working now and provide 2x, 5x, or 10x the *value* you offer to customers.

As we continued talking, I asked the owners if they were familiar with all the dance crazes happening on social media. You know what I'm talking about. Scroll through your social media feed and half the videos are of individuals, families, or even teams of people dancing.

"What if you did this?" I asked. "What if you charged a company $10,000 to teach their employees how to do a dance and then filmed that routine at their place of business? Would that be hard?" I asked.

"No," they said. "That's what we do. We teach people how to dance."

"Yeah," I continued, "but if you teach a little kid to dance, you get $250 over six weeks and you have to pay for the building. But if you teach a corporate team to dance, that is worth a lot more.

Corporations are looking for team-building activities. Not only that, if you film the video at their place of work and they use it on social media, it's great advertising. It's a great recruiting tool too because everybody wants to work at a place with a fun culture."

Think about what we just did. We figured out how our friends who run a dance studio could do the exact same work and charge fivefold or more. For a large company, this would be a cost-effective team-building exercise as well as good advertising and a good recruiting tool. Ten thousand dollars is a steal for that kind of value, and the dance studio just increased the value of their product dramatically without increasing the cost of the product itself at all.

Another guest on the podcast, a wedding planner out of Chicago, was challenged with growing her business without having to duplicate herself. She charged quite a bit for each wedding but because she was only one person, was limited in her ability to scale. During the interview, we optimized her product offering by creating a product called *Plan Your Own Wedding*. For $5K, she would walk you through a robust checklist by giving you access to step-by-step videos that helped couples plan everything from the event space to catering to flowers and even cocktail recipes. Not only this, but when customers signed up for the step-by-step process they got to meet, in a cohort, with her each week for 90 minutes to ask questions and address concerns. Suddenly our wedding planner went from planning one wedding at a time to planning 10 or 15. And all it cost her was 90 minutes each week. She could plan 10 weddings in a fraction of the time she could previously plan one, and if anybody wanted to upgrade to her personal services, they could pay for her previous service.

Another idea for enlarging the wings of your airplane is concierge service. I once had a doctor who charged me a monthly fee to be a "member" of his program. The idea was that he promised to have many fewer clients and take more time with each of them. I still had to pay a fee whenever I went to see him, but when I did we'd sit in his office for an hour or more and talk about diet and exercise and health trends and family history. I never once felt rushed. Was it expensive? It was but I cared enough about my health and longevity that the fee was worth it.

Is it possible to make the wings of your airplane stronger, lighter, and larger? For almost everybody reading this book, it is. You can charge a premium for more focused attention. You can bundle products together to create packages of products. You can take some of your expertise online and coach people in groups. You can charge a monthly fee for information you have access to. Even if you represent somebody else's products and there's nothing you can do to change that, you can offer a subscription service where folks get the product monthly.

So how do we optimize our product offering?

There are three exercises you can conduct to optimize your product offering. The first is to rate your products for profit. In this exercise you're going to look at your current offering and get brutally honest about what's bringing in money and what's weighing your airplane down. This exercise will help you focus your marketing and sales energy for optimum profit.

The second exercise involves a product brainstorm in which you see if you can offer new products that will bring in more revenue and profit. This exercise will expand the surface area of your wings.

The third exercise involves using a product brief to decide what products you should create to grow your business. A product brief is a form you fill out every time you have a new product idea. This form will help you realize whether or not the new product is a good idea or whether you'd be wasting valuable time, costs, and energy trying to bring it into the world.

When you perform these three exercises, and continue to perform them on a regular basis, you will improve your airplane by making sure the wings are optimized for lift. These exercises, by the way, are the secret to many multibillion-dollar businesses. Entire research and development processes, boards, and committees are in constant motion to create new and better products allowing them to keep pace with the competition and serve the ever-changing needs of their customers. Even though you are a small business, you can implement similar processes to optimize your product offering for revenue and profit.

Step One: Rate Your Products for Profitability

In the day-to-day whirlwind of running a business, we often lose track of which products are making us money and which products are weighing down our airplane. Selling products that are not profitable is like strapping two-by-fours to the side of our airplane and expecting them to work like wings. Your airplane won't get any lift. In fact, any product that is not profitable is creating serious drag on your airplane while simultaneously stressing your right and left engines. In order for your airplane's wings to remain light and strong, your products should be profitable and in demand.

Sometimes a product can be sold at a loss because it brings in customers who may buy more profitable products, but these instances are the exception to the rule.

The first exercise we will conduct to both lighten and strengthen the wings of our airplane involves ranking our products in order of profitability, from most to least profitable. Conducting this exercise brings us face-to-face with the truth about which products are really paying the bills.

If you have a retail store that sells hundreds or thousands of products, this exercise may be too involved. That said, you can easily rank your fifty best-selling products, which you will likely find account for 50 percent to 80 percent of your revenue anyway.

The exercise of ranking your products for profitability is going to do two important things for you as a small-business owner: It's going to show you where your money is really coming from, and it's going to inform you about where to spend more of your marketing and sales effort.

When you rank your products by profitability, ask the following questions:

1. How much do your raw materials cost?
2. How much of your labor costs are directly related to the creation, marketing, and sales of this product?
3. Does the product expire and, if so, how does expiring and unsold inventory affect the cost of your product?

Ultimately the number you are looking for is the difference between what you sell a product for and what it costs to produce, support, and sell that product. This is a little different from "cost of goods sold," but the idea is the same.

It's important to note this is not an official accounting exercise. You aren't turning this form in to the government or even to your accountant (although it's not a bad idea to have your accountant provide their input). This exercise is purely about gaining an awareness of how your company makes money.

Here's the process you should go through to rate your products:

1. List every product you sell on a whiteboard or piece of paper—if you're a retailer that has thousands of products, try to list your top 50 or so.
2. Use your gut instinct to list those products in rank order for profitability.
3. Do due diligence to make sure your list is right—truly figure out how profitable your products actually are.

If it's possible to do this exercise with your leadership team, feel free. Your team will have different perspectives on which products are profitable and which products are not.

Use the Product Profitability Audit in your Small Business Flight Plan to conduct exercise one.

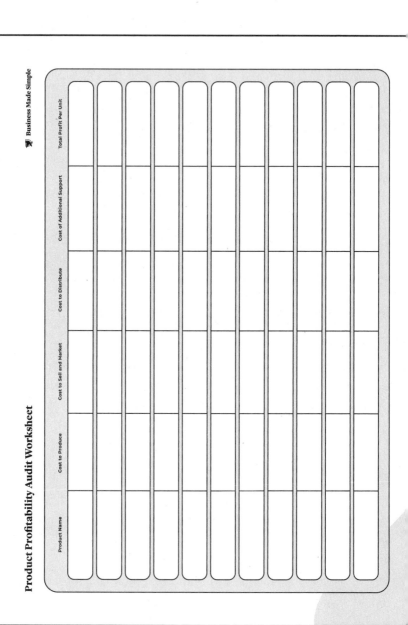

Product Profitability Audit Worksheet

Business Made Simple

Product Name	Cost to Produce	Cost to Sell and Market	Cost to Distribute	Cost of Additional Support	Total Profit Per Unit

Access a digital, fillable version at SmallBusinessFlightPlan.com

After we know where our business really makes money and where it doesn't, we need to ask ourselves some difficult questions:

1. How much bandwidth is being used producing, marketing, and distributing products that are not very profitable?
2. Can we stop selling some of those products?
3. Are the marketing and sales efforts reflective of our profitability ranking?
4. How can we allot more marketing and sales resources to increase sales on our highest-profit items?

Can You Sell More of What's Already Working?

As small-business owners, we often make the mistake of believing our path to greater revenue must involve creating and selling new products. That logic makes sense. We launch one product, it starts to sell, we enjoy the positive cash flow, and we want to duplicate our efforts with another product. Repeat.

But that only makes sense if we've reached market saturation. The truth is, most small businesses haven't saturated the market.

If we can sell more of the high-profit products we are already selling, let's try that before doing all the work to create and launch a new product. In other words, let's make the fire bigger by pouring gas on what's already burning!

The money you need to grow your company may be sitting right in front of you. Is your pet store making great profit on a specific brand of dog food? Double your next order and turn it into an end-cap display, feature that bag of dog food in your next email, stack it high in the store window and have your retail team mention how great that particular brand of dog food is to every person who comes in to buy a chew toy.

If you are known for selling a specific product, it's much easier to sell more of that product than become known for selling something else. Both are possible, of course, but selling more of what you're already selling is easier.

Can You Let Go of Products That Are Not Bringing You a Profit?

Now that we've doubled down on what's working, let's consider letting go of the products that aren't selling.

Sometimes, of course, this is difficult and maybe even unwise to do. You may not make much money off a pack of gum, but folks who come into the store to buy gum often buy a large soft drink, which is very profitable. Excluding those loss leaders or break-even leaders, though, there are certainly products you can ditch that are taking up too much mental and financial energy. What would happen if you cut those products and focused your marketing on what's already working?

In storytelling, there is a famous phrase that applies just as strongly to business: Kill your darlings. This phrase has helped create many literary masterpieces and can help your business take off, too.

I can't emphasize this enough: If you can cut products and streamline your product offering, do it today.

Step Two: Add New, Profitable Products to Your Product Offering

When you stop spending valuable marketing and sales resources on products that don't bring in a profit and reassign those resources to products that do make you money, the wings of your airplane become larger and your airplane generates more lift. Optimizing the performance of your wings by ranking your products and assigning more sales and marketing resources to what's already working is the first step. The second step is to create more products that are as profitable or more profitable than your highest performers.

When you're dreaming up a new product, consider this question first: What can I bring to market that will provide the most value to my customer?

There are many categories of products where people will pay a premium, but here are the six categories of problems and product offerings most successful companies produce and categories you can explore to expand your product offering:

1. **Making Money:** If the product you sell will help people make money, it's worth money. If you sell a franchise, for instance, you're selling a business that people can run and make a great living from. If you wholesale products that other people can sell, you're helping people make money. Financial advice, coaching, and sales representation are all products that help other people make money. Marketing and advertising are great examples of investments people make in order to get a financial return. If you're

selling certification so people can better represent your brand, or training on how to invest or sell, you are able to charge a premium because, in the end, you're a direct financial investment in which your customer will get a good return.

2. **Saving Money:** If your product saves customers money, they will pay you a percentage of that savings. For instance, if you sell solar panels that will, over the years, save your customer thousands in energy bills, you can charge a percentage of that savings. If you are able to broker a deal and save your client money, you can charge a percentage of that savings.

3. **Reducing Frustrations:** If your product is able to alleviate stress and anxiety, you have a great product to sell. People will pay for a sense of peace, calm, and resolution. The frustrations people experience most include a lack of time, a lack of organization, or a lack of knowledge. Services as simple as dog walking fit into this category along with more elevated services such as therapy or counseling.

4. **Gaining Status:** If you have a luxury item or product that includes limited access, people will invest in your brand. Rolex sells a watch that is about the same quality as many other watches but people buy them as a way of acknowledging their success or achievement. A luxury car, a penthouse suite, even a special table at a restaurant are examples of premium products that carry with them an elevated sense of status.

5. **Creating Connection:** If you are able to create a community of like-minded individuals, you have a

terrific product opportunity for which there is a human longing. The desire for human connection with others experiencing similar challenges or ambitions is a valuable commodity.

6. **Offering Simplicity:** When a customer has a problem, they don't just want to solve the problem, they want to solve the problem as easily and simply as possible. If you have an all-in service that can solve your customer's problem with one easy payment or perhaps a subscription method, you've got a great product. Most subscription services fit into this category. If you're mowing my lawn or cleaning up my book, you're simplifying my life. For that, I will pay a premium.

Three Proven Places to Create Profitable Revenue Starting Now

Now that we know six types of offerings that are always in demand, we must determine how we can package those offerings as products that deliver the most value and have the greatest positive effect on the bottom line of our business. Here are three great ideas:

1. **Subscriptions:** Whether you sell paper towels, financial advice, pet food, or even human food, turn your product offering into a daily, weekly, or monthly subscription. Allow your customers to choose how often they want to receive a forty-pound bag of dog food and start shipping it on a schedule. For them, this amounts to incredible convenience; for you, it amounts to a steady stream of profitable income.

2. **Certifications:** If you're selling an expertise, consider duplicating yourself in the form of a certification. Yes, you can certify people on nearly any expertise that can be leveraged into a small (or large) business. Have you spent the last twenty years consulting with wannabe home gardeners? Leverage your expertise into a home gardening consultant certification.

3. **Package deals:** Often your customers don't just come to you to buy a product, they come to you to solve a problem. For instance, if you own a store that sells greeting cards, paper products, and party supplies, consider packing a "Children's Birthday Party Package" that includes banners, paper plates, hats, and so on. Customers who come in to buy some balloons and a banner will discover that their entire problem (How do I decorate for my child's birthday party?) can be solved in one simple purchase. If you are going to create package deals, start with the top three problems customers seek you out to solve and create packages around those problems. For instance, the "New Puppy Package" is great for a pet store and the "Best Valentine's Day Ever" travel package would be terrific for any travel agent. Get creative. Just remember, your customers aren't seeking you out to buy a product, they're seeking you out to solve a problem! Organize the solution to that problem into a package and watch your sales increase.

Step Three: Install a Product Brief

One of the great things about running a small business is you get to implement decisions quickly. A service can suddenly exist today that didn't exist yesterday. Larger businesses are bogged down in committees and market testing, but not you.

Well, I've got not-so-good news for you. Or perhaps it's good news. It depends on how you look at it. The news is this: Those product-creating processes exist for a reason. As you get larger, the freewheeling entrepreneurial spirit can slow you down because the more people there are in the business, the harder the business is to pivot. When a business is larger and the visionary leader starts making fast decisions, half the team has no idea the business went in a new direction and confusion and frustration abound.

The answer, even for small businesses, is to start using product briefs.

As a freewheeling visionary entrepreneur, the idea of installing product briefs into your business may sound about as beneficial as pouring pancake syrup into an engine. I get it. When our business started using product briefs, I was convinced the process would gum up the process and slow us down. Here's the thing: The purpose of a product brief is to create doubt. Doubt, it turns out, is your friend. If you and your team's ideas can make it through the gauntlet of questioning involved in a product brief, the idea is much more likely to evolve and ultimately positively affect the bottom line. Failing to fill out a product brief as a way of vetting your ideas, however, will ultimately slow your business down with bad products that hit the market with a thud.

Filling out a product brief launches a process in which you and your team spend a week or two doing due diligence before launching a product or service. During the product brief, you and/or your team analyze whether launching the new idea will interfere with existing revenue streams, confuse customers, be profitable and sustainable, or bloat your overhead (the body of the airplane)—causing more harm than good.

For you high-control folks who like to run-and-gun and install the wings of the airplane while it's barreling down the runway, trust me: Slowing down to install a product brief is going to grow your business a little bit slower but a heck of a lot bigger.

Our run-and-gun ways might make us feel free, but the truth is we're leaving a pile of frustration behind us as we go. When we decide to create a "new product" then pivot a week later and forget we even brought up the idea a month later, we run the risk of burning out our team. Not only this, but failing to slow down and analyze our plan and do due diligence about its potential amounts to amateur hour. If you ever want to sell your company, investors and buyers will smell the lack of professionalism about halfway through the second analysis meeting and realize the processes you have in place are entirely dependent on you and cannot be duplicated. This will devalue your business.

Performing a product brief process is necessary if you want to professionalize your operation.

I know a business owner who made his entire team so angry that they got together and collectively wrote him a letter saying he was too spontaneous and inconsistent to work for and spelled out a few processes that would make their jobs (serving him) easier. His response was to fire his entire staff. Some of his team members had served him faithfully for ten years. To this day, he refuses to speak to them. The result? He is surrounded by a new team of underpaid, submissive servants who will not give him honest feedback for fear of retaliation. As a result, he consistently makes a fool of himself with his public speculations about what he will offer. His business is limited. Even though his business has a hundred-million-dollar potential, it will never grow past three to four million dollars.

Those of us who need high levels of control hate product briefs. I know because I used to be a control freak myself. To be honest, I'd still be a control freak if I hadn't discovered my team members are actually smarter than I am, are in closer relationships with many of my customers, and remember better than I do the mistakes we've made in the past. I do not submit to product briefs because I am a good boss and business owner (though I hope to be). I submit to product briefs because they are a foundational process for building a better, more profitable business.

The sort of feedback I get from product briefs looks something like this: If we implemented the proposed idea, we would not be consistent with our big announcement at the beginning of the year. We would confuse customers about who we are and what we do. Worse, we'd take necessary work hours away from the creation of our most profitable products in order to experiment with this new idea.

I have also seen a product brief greatly enhance an already good idea.

The point is this: The product brief gives me valuable feedback before I spend time and money (overhead) bringing that product to market.

Getting negative feedback doesn't always mean an idea should be tabled. Often, pushback provides a valuable list of risks that should be mitigated before an initiative is launched.

Each new idea, whether it's a product, a service, or a marketing plan is a brick in the wall of your business. If you run-and-gun, you will build your business much faster but many of the bricks will be half-baked and cracked. Yes, a product brief will slow down the day-to-day feel of the business but when you implement the brief, your business will grow stronger and be more dependable.

When engineers design an airplane, they test wing designs in wind tunnels before ever installing them on an airplane. Slight tweaks in the design can result in better fuel economy, greater lift, and less drag. Without the wind tunnel, the entire plane would have to be built in order to test the wings. This would drive up costs enormously if a guessed-on design actually had to be pulled back and redesigned, or worse, scrapped altogether.

Put your products through the wind tunnel of the product brief before launching those products.

Use Product Briefs for Any Important Initiative

Product briefs can be used for more than just products. At my company, we are just as likely to use a product brief for a new marketing initiative as we are for a new product. When I look back on all the failed marketing attempts I've thrown to my marketing team before we had product briefs, I wonder at how much time we wasted experimenting with ideas that could have been "tested" via the product brief worksheet.

If you want to create products that sell, marketing initiatives that work, and a company culture that is stable, install a product brief process today.

The Product Brief Worksheet

The Product Profitability Audit and the Product Brief Worksheet are both in your Small Business Flight Plan.

Product Brief Worksheet   🦉 **Business Made Simple**

Project Owner: _____

PRODUCT NAME

1. What is the product name? _____

2. Does it describe the product well and tease the value?
   _____

3. Will the name be confusing or create a problem in the marketplace?
   _____
   _____

PRODUCT DESCRIPTION

1. What problem does this product solve for our customer?
   _____

2. How does the product resolve the customer's problem?
   _____

3. Describe the benefits the customer will experience if they use the product:
   _____
   _____

4. Describe the features of this product and how it's going to help customers:
   _____
   _____

CORE MESSAGING

1. Who are we selling this to?
   _____

2. Do we have access to the target market for this product, and if so, how?
   _____
   _____

3. How will we define the customer's problem for marketing collateral?
   _____
   _____

Access a digital, fillable version at SmallBusinessFlightPlan.com

4. What is our one-liner?

HIGH-LEVEL MARKETING RESEARCH

1. Is there a proven demand for this product in the marketplace?

2. Have we sent out a customer survey ensuring our customers would want this product? What questions did we ask in the survey and what were the results?

3. If we offer this product, who will we be competing with?

    a. Are we priced above or below the competition?

    b. How are we positioned against the competition? (What makes our product better?)

FINANCIALS

1. What is the price of this product and how did we determine this price?

2. Will it be profitable?

3. How much will this cost us to build? How much will this cost us to maintain? (Do we need to hire support staff, more tech support, etc?)

4. Who will be responsible for revenue related to this product?

SALES PROJECTIONS (BASED ON CURRENT CUSTOMER BASE)

1. What are the 30-60-90-day sales goals?

2. What's the first-year revenue projection related to this product?

3. What's the goal for units sold in the first year?

PRODUCT VALIDATION

1. Will this product cause any problems with existing products?

2. Will this product upset any existing or future customers? Why?

KEY DATES

1. When will this product be launched?

2. When will the landing page for this product be created?

3. When will the prerelease announcement be made to current customers?

SALES AND MARKETING PLAN

1. When will we check off the key sales and marketing components of this product?

    a. One-liner: _____

    b. Landing page: _____

    c. Lead generator: _____

    d. Nurture or sales emails: _____

    e. Social collateral: _____

Depending on the product or marketing initiative you are introducing, not every question in the Product Brief Worksheet will apply. Use the questions that do apply to spark thoughtful conversation about this important business decision and ignore the rest.

Your Products Determine Your Progress and Your Profit

Again, most business leaders don't think about optimizing their product offering but launching the right new product can be a fast way of improving the bottom line.

If you do the following three things, the wings of your airplane will be optimized and your business will grow:

1. Rank your products for profitability; consider letting go of products that are not profitable and/or in demand.
2. Introduce new products to your customers that increase your revenue and profit.
3. Install a product brief that ensures new products and initiatives are a success.

Once we've set our business on a mission, ramped up our marketing and sales engines, and created lift for our business by optimizing our product offering, it's time to slim down the body of our airplane. The next step in growing your business involves using a management and productivity playbook. For those of you who struggle to align your team and who wonder if your team members actually know what they're supposed to be doing, our *Management and Productivity Made Simple Playbook* is going to solve your problem.

5

Overhead and Operations

STEP FIVE: The Body

Streamline Your Overhead and Operations with Management and Productivity Made Simple

Step Five Will Help You Solve These Problems:

- Too many people are wearing too many hats.
- Team members aren't getting consistent feedback.
- Your culture feels like organized chaos.
- Your leaders need better management skills.
- You have too many meetings and they aren't productive.
- Your team members aren't nearly as focused as they could be.

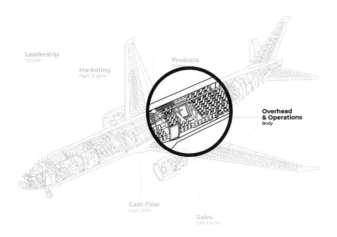

Leadership
Cockpit

Marketing
Right Engine

Products
Wings

Overhead
& Operations
Body

Cash Flow
Fuel Tanks

Sales
Left Engine

.   .   .

I f the body of an airplane is too large to be supported by the wings and the engines, the plane will crash. That's why when you board one of those smaller commuter planes you have to duck your head to get in the door. There's a reason airplanes look like flying pencils. It's because the shape, size, and weight of the body must be as lean and streamlined as possible to mitigate the plane's need for power, lift, and fuel.

Our small businesses work the same way. The products we sell and the sales and marketing efforts that move those products should compensate (and, hopefully, overcompensate) for the overhead necessary to run our day-to-day operations.

If you want an airplane to fly, make the wings wide, the right and left engines powerful, and the body of the airplane streamlined and light. In other words, if you want your small business to make money, make the marketing and sales engines powerful, make the product profitable, and keep overhead down!

So the question is: How to we keep our overhead lean?

If you had to cut your overhead by 20 percent tomorrow, where would you start? Many of us would look over our credit card statements or start listing the monthly subscription services we never use. And those are perfectly great places to start, but saving money is only part of the equation. For most small businesses, those things aren't where your overhead bloat is coming from. The reality is your largest expenses aren't monthly subscriptions or that sales rep running around with the company credit card.

For most small businesses, out-of-control overhead comes from a single place: labor.

Creeping overhead can sink a business. Technology and rent can be expensive, too, but it's labor that will crash a plane faster than anything else. The biggest expense has always been labor. Even if you're a solo-preneur, you're likely relying on freelancers and vendors to do the heavy lifting, and labor is likely causing the body of your airplane to expand faster than a balloon at a birthday party.

As I meet with small-business owners, I hear a similar story as it relates to overhead: The business was doing well so the owner hired a few people to help; then the cost of labor was more than they anticipated. Plus, managing the new people took them out of their sweet spot. Once the owner was out of their sweet spot, sales slowed a bit but the cost of labor remained the same and then, as the nose of the plane started to dip, everybody that had just been hired had to be let go.

If labor is the biggest expense affecting overhead, then how do we cut overhead? We might suppose that letting people go is the answer.

In fact, when turnaround teams go into big companies to stabilize a spiraling airplane, the very first thing they do is analyze labor and start laying people off. Downgrading office space and streamlining technology doesn't happen for months because it's labor, dreaded labor, that is usually the problem.

If you want to decrease the weight of your airplane and streamline the body, open the emergency doors and start throwing seats into the clouds. The fewer people in the body of the airplane, the better. Sadly, for many of us small-business owners, this means getting rid of your aunt who does the accounting, your best friend from high school who helps with your technology, and your nephew out back who cleans all those parts before they get transferred to welding.

Cutting payroll often means cutting off relationships with the people you love, being disowned by your family, and becoming that greedy capitalist who only cares about themselves and their money. I know it's tough, but you have to do it and you have to do it fast. In the pursuit of greatness we have to be coldhearted, don't we?

Not so fast.

If you can streamline your labor force with a management and productivity playbook that transforms all those seats in the body of the plane to high-functioning additions to the wings and engines, the rest of your airplane would grow in proportion so that it matched the body. What if, instead of letting everybody go, your entire labor force became a business-building group of focused professionals that contributed mightily to the bottom line? It means your business would start growing and your overhead would transform into an investment rather than a spend.

Yes, it's important to review your credit card bills and cancel some of those monthly subscriptions, but, make no mistake, the number one thing you can do to streamline your overhead and get your pencil-thin airplane moving through the air so fast the paint rips off the fuselage is to install a *Management and Productivity Playbook.*

The playbook I will give you in this chapter won't decrease your overhead right away. If your airplane is currently taking a nosedive, you may have to let some people go. I hate that but there are times laying people off is necessary to save the plane itself. If you've got a little time before you run out of money, though, we can streamline your workforce so work gets done in less time and the work itself is focused on the three economic priorities you defined in your Mission Statement. This, in turn, may save your business from crashing.

When your labor is focused on your three economic priorities, more money will flow into the business itself. This in turn allows the wings, engines, fuel tanks, and cockpit to catch up with your bloated overhead. The best way to decrease the size of the body of your airplane is not to decrease it at all, but to make the rest of the airplane larger while your payroll stays exactly the same (save for commissions for your sales reps and profit-based bonuses, which will hopefully increase).

Even if you aren't having a problem with your overhead expenses, installing a management and productivity playbook is a good idea for many reasons. Optimizing your workflow will increase your profit, energize your team, and increase morale. Also, your customers will get more focused attention, and your products and services will increase in quality.

The Seemingly Unsolvable Problem

When I first started my small business, we didn't need a management and productivity playbook. I only had one team member, and we'd simply touch base every morning to talk about what we were going to work on that day. The system was seamless and efficient. Then, we hired another team member. To be sure, a third team member added a layer of complexity but because we were all working out of the same tiny office, communication was terrific, and we were rarely confused about what we were supposed to be working on.

As the business grew, we added a couple freelance designers, then coders, and then copywriters and videographers. As you likely know, when a few of your team members (freelancers or otherwise) work remotely, it becomes more difficult to align the workflow. At one point I remember overhearing a phone conversation only to realize one of our contract workers had spent the previous week working on a project we'd canceled the previous month. That entire week's work was lost. That's the real way overhead gets out of hand—when you have team members doing work that does not support the economic priorities of the business. If that sort of thing gets out of control, the business will crash.

Sadly, most small businesses never realize the body of the airplane is getting too heavy. As leaders, we sit in the cockpit dialing up destinations and plotting our course while the folks in the rest of the plane wonder where this thing is going and why. Because they are good people, they work hard and even create work when they aren't given clear objectives. If we aren't careful we can easily end up flying a plane full of team members doing busy work.

To make sure everybody on the team was well managed, I promoted one of our leaders to Chief of Staff and that helped, but this individual had never been in that position before and without a formal system, the results were mixed. There always seemed to be a disconnect between the cockpit and body because the leaders in the cockpit were too busy plotting the course and filling the fuel tanks. Because we didn't meet regularly with our team members and give them an actual playbook to run, our efforts to steady the plane didn't work. We still had team members running around not quite sure what they were supposed to be working on.

Once we realized we couldn't solve the problem ourselves, we hired an executive from a large company to help, but that was a mistake. Most large businesses solve problems like these by throwing enormous amounts of money at them. When you have a billion-dollar budget, that's great, but it never works with a small business. Small businesses need to operate lean and don't have time to form boards and run test groups and perfect hiring practices and so on and so forth. We small-business owners can't afford the waste that a large corporation has built into the margins.

When hiring specialists didn't work, we began to interview consultants from a number of management and productivity companies. To hire a consultant that could help us install lean management or some other productivity system ran as high as $100,000 per year. We didn't have that kind of money to spare.

The solutions we researched were complex and, moreover, seemed designed for much larger organizations than ours. At that time, we employed about twelve people, along with a dozen or so contract workers. The management and productivity systems available to us were built for businesses whose employees numbered in the hundreds, if not thousands.

What we really needed was a management and productivity playbook for small business.

"Management and Productivity Made Simple" to the Rescue

It wasn't until my friend, Doug Keim, stepped into the cockpit that we began to streamline our workflow. Doug is an old friend who came over from a larger corporation as a favor. I'd known him as a mentor for a few years and, even though he'd spent the majority of his career turning around multibillion-dollar companies, he took an interest in me and my small business. When he finished a three-year turnaround at a big company in Atlanta, I asked him if he'd be willing to spend a year with us to create a management and productivity playbook for small businesses. I explained to Doug that we'd need to create this playbook from scratch; it simply didn't exist out there in the corporate world. "Most small businesses are making it up as they go along." Doug understood and thought he might enjoy the challenge. Under his leadership, we designed a management and productivity system that we used in our own business.

We called the playbook *The Management and Productivity Made Simple Playbook* because it was simple to install, simple to use, and, more importantly, it worked.

It was amazing to watch Doug work. He spent all of his time in the body of the airplane, helping everybody clarify their objectives and overcome challenges. His personality worked more like a basketball coach than an executive. He'd huddle with the team, draw up plays, and then set them free on the court for a few minutes—allowing them to use their intuition within the boundaries of a set of objectives. When the team freewheeled a little too much, he'd call them back over, remind them of the objectives, ask if they had any feedback or wanted to evolve the plan a bit, make whatever changes he felt were positive, and then send them back out on the court.

Finally, my company began to grow. Not only did the company grow, but it grew during a season when it should have shrunk—if not gone under completely. When we brought Doug on, we were 75 percent dependent upon people getting on airplanes and attending our marketing and sales workshops. Only a few months after Doug joined the team and began to install our new *Management and Productivity Playbook*, the COVID pandemic shut down most of the world. We watched as the virus shut down an entire region of China and started hearing rumors the same thing would happen in America. That scenario seemed implausible to me, but friends started calling saying their brother, uncle, or niece worked at the State Department or were in the National Guard, and they were hearing cryptic rumors. I realized pretty quickly that regardless of what was true, the economic ecosystem was about to be disrupted.

My mind was split. Half of me believed our little airplane could miraculously stay in the air while the other half was trying to find a lake or pond we could use to water-land.

How did an in-person coaching company survive a global pandemic in which travel was brought to a halt? *Management and Productivity Made Simple* came to the rescue.

We'd already established our three main economic priorities. That move alone helped to streamline our workflow more than anything else we'd done in the history of the company. Using the new *Management and Productivity Made Simple Playbook*, we broke the twelve months following the shutdown into three-week sprints, each week supporting one of the economic priorities. We transitioned from in-person events to online workshops (something our clients had been asking us to do for years anyway) and revised our marketing messages to focus on a relevant value offer: surviving the pandemic. I confess the pandemic tightened our focus and added a sense of urgency. During our leadership meetings we summoned the focus and intensity of a team trying to win a national championship. We reminded ourselves of our three economic priorities, we defined and owned our different assignments, and we went back to work for at least one more day—if nothing else.

The results were surprising. When our small business should have crash-landed into a cattle pond in Kansas, we grew by more than 20 percent in revenue and nearly 30 percent in profit. We didn't lay off a single team member and even added contractors to help with the workload. We tripled our rainy-day fund (think of this as adding a thousand pounds of fuel to the reserve fuel tank, all while in the air) and handed out bonuses at the end of the year. The playbook worked. Because the playbook worked so well, we still use it today, and I believe we will be using it twenty years from now—no matter how big we get.

The *Management and Productivity Made Simple Playbook* can be used by any small business to streamline their workflow, increase productivity (and revenue), and boost the morale that so often suffers when people aren't properly coached and encouraged.

Install the *Management and Productivity Made Simple Playbook*

To use the *Management and Productivity Made Simple Playbook*, all you have to do is begin to hold five separate meetings. I know that sounds like a lot of meetings considering you're probably attending too many meetings already, but these meetings are designed to replace most of the meetings that are currently bogging you down, some of the five meetings last as little as five minutes, and you, the leader of the business, will not have to attend all of them.

In fact, as the leader of my small business, the number of meetings (internal) I had to attend was cut in half when we created and started to implement the playbook. I have more, not less, free time because of it. Our meetings are fixed on a set schedule, so I was able to establish a repeating cadence that created a manageable work flow. Not only this, but during this same season, my wife and I added our first child. I truly believe without the *Management and Productivity Made Simple Playbook* I would not have been as present as I have been as a husband and father. I love my new schedule and believe we've set ourselves up for years of business growth. Not only this, but the playbook contributes positively to my personal and family health.

The Five Meetings

Later in this chapter I'll give you an actual playbook as well as meeting templates that will streamline your operations. For now, though, here is a brief description of the five meetings we engage in as a team.

The All-Staff Meeting

Every Monday at 10:00 a.m. the entire staff gets together; some attend in person and some virtually. The purpose of this meeting is threefold:

1. Maintain alignment and focus around the three economic priorities,
2. Update the entire team about any department initiatives or successes, and
3. Keep morale up by publicly honoring team members who are demonstrating exceptional work that helps your team make progress toward your three economic priorities.

The All-Staff Meeting is your longest meeting, from 45 minutes to an hour. The energy for this meeting should be high and helps you create a family-like atmosphere. A specific template should be filled out before the meeting. This template ensures the meeting is thoughtfully planned so it contributes to the economic priorities.

The Leadership Meeting

The Leadership Meeting takes place right after the All-Staff Meeting. This meeting consists of department heads and is designed to talk about the primary initiatives currently in motion as well as address any roadblocks that are holding back your economic objectives. This meeting usually lasts a half hour to an hour, depending on how many initiatives your team needs to cover that week.

The Leadership Meeting Template should be used to plan this meeting. The template will be filled out by you or the team member in charge of the meeting. Filling out the template makes sure each Leadership Meeting helps the overall company achieve the three current economic priorities.

The Department Stand-up

If your small business has more than five or six team members and those team members are divided into two or three departments, you may want to begin holding Department Stand-ups. If your team is smaller than two or three team members, an All-Staff Meeting or Leadership Meeting may be all you need. That said, you'll want to hold that All-Staff Meeting more than once each week and likely three or four times each week. On Monday, hold a longer meeting but on the other days, keep it short and use the Department Stand-up Template to guide the meeting. As your team grows, though, you will want each department to hold Department Stand-ups each morning that there is no All-Staff Meeting.

Department Stand-up Meetings last for less than fifteen minutes and help ensure each department is working on an initiative or initiatives that support the three economic priorities of the business. It is during this meeting that department leaders set the objectives for the coming day and address any roadblocks team members may be experiencing regarding the previous day's workflow. A Department Stand-up Template is filled out before the meeting.

The Personal Priority Speed Check

As your team continues to grow, each new team member is going to want to know how well they are doing their job. Ongoing coaching is critical to keep productivity and morale high.

Once you have five or ten people on your team and the overall team is divided into separate departments, each director should meet one-on-one with their individual team members each week in a Personal Priority Speed Check. These meetings also last about fifteen minutes and are designed to zoom in on each person's responsibilities within the context of their team. The Personal Priority Speed Check Template is filled out by the team member him/herself before the meeting. This template ensures the meeting has been thoughtfully planned so each team member feels supported as they contribute to the economic priorities of the overall business.

While this meeting may seem like too much to add to your workflow, remember two things: The meeting only lasts fifteen minutes per team member and your department leaders (not you) are holding these meetings.

Because your department heads are giving each team member the individual attention they need, your team members will feel supported and you will experience a surge in morale.

If you are a solo-preneur, of course, this meeting will not be necessary but it can be a great way to hold yourself accountable to your own economic and personal priorities. That said, if you do have a small staff, consider holding the Personal Priority Speed Check once each week (or at least once each month) with each individual team member. Use the Personal Priority Speed Check Template to guide the meeting and make sure your team member has filled it out before the meeting. You will be amazed how much time is saved, rather than wasted, by holding these meetings. Not only this, but your team will respect you all the more for giving them the individual attention they crave—even if it's only fifteen minutes each week.

Quarterly Performance Reviews

So far, our meetings have revolved around generating focus and productivity. We haven't however, addressed performance.

In the Quarterly Performance Review you will carefully assess each team member's performance. You'll ask questions like: Are they often late? Is the quality of their work subpar? How might management help them improve? These conversations are a mix between management and coaching in which each of your directors help their team members understand how to improve in their professional career. If you like, the fourth-quarter performance review can also be tied to a bonus and pay structure.

Your Quarterly Performance Reviews address the number one question most team members have: Am I doing a good job? These meetings are mostly positive but because they are a little longer and because the Quarterly Performance Review Template is filled out by both the team member and department head, an honest conversation is fostered and a natural, healthy environment for coaching and improvement is created.

As is suggested by the title, the Quarterly Performance Reviews take place once each quarter.

The Five Meetings That Will Transform Your Company and Streamline Your Overhead and Operations

These are the five meetings that will grow your small business. There are other meetings, of course, but, as you grow, if you implement the All-Staff, Leadership, Department Stand-up, Personal Priority Speed Check, and Quarterly Performance Review meetings, the flow of important information from person-to-person will not be blocked, and efficiency will increase.

When I talk about efficiency, I'm talking about the flow of energy to the wings and engines. Energy used to enlarge the wings or increase the thrust of the engines creates more income for the business and so can be considered an investment, whereas energy used within the body of the airplane (while often necessary for administrative tasks) should be considered a spend because it does not translate directly to revenue creation.

When team-member energy contributes to the wings and the engines, it does not count against the size and weight of the body; therefore, the *Management and Productivity Made Simple Playbook* is designed to move energy stuck in the body of the airplane out onto the wings and into the engines, thus decreasing the overhead-drag versus lift-thrust ratio.

This exact playbook may not work perfectly for you. Feel free to use the templates, though, to create a hybrid management and productivity playbook of your own. I assure you this playbook will work a lot better than many of the six-figure consulting systems firms will attempt to bring into your business.

Are These the Meetings That Replace Most Meetings?

You may look at these five meetings and feel resistance. How could you add anymore meetings to your existing schedule? I get it. Again, though, these meetings are designed to replace all those "can we get together?" meetings that are bogging down your schedule.

Not only this, but as the owner of the company or the person running the company, only three of these meetings are meetings you'll attend personally: The All-Staff, Leadership, and (some of) the Quarterly Performance Reviews. The rest of the meetings are run by department directors.

The *Management and Productivity Made Simple Playbook* isn't just designed to streamline leadership and management meetings; it's designed to increase focus and decrease meetings for every single team member. Will you never have an out-of-the-playbook meeting because you've installed the *Management and Productivity Made Simple Playbook*? Sadly, no. You will continue to have outside meetings with customers, staff, leaders of other companies, and vendors, but you'll be able to attend those meetings knowing your business is not losing focus because of your absence. That will make those outside meetings more pleasurable. In fact, you'll find yourself being fully present in those outside meetings because things are running so smoothly at home.

Who Should Run the Management and Productivity Playbook?

Another concern you may have is that these five meetings will take an enormous amount of time to implement. If you felt that concern in your bones as you read about these meetings, you likely aren't the person who should install the *Management and Productivity Made Simple Playbook*. Not everybody is wired to run a management and productivity playbook. In fact, if I had to install the playbook in my own company, we likely would never have implemented it at all, and my company would have suffered.

I assure you it's not because this isn't a good playbook. I think the playbook is exceptionally simple and effective. The reason I would never have installed it is because I am not an operator—I'm an artist/entrepreneur.

Of the three kinds of leaders you normally find at the top of a successful small business, there is the artist, the entrepreneur, and the operator.

The Artist

The artist obsesses over products and product creation. They care about how a product works, whether or not customers are happy with it, and how it is brought to market. The artist is often a visionary who "sees the future" as it relates to the business and how their products will affect their customers. Without the artist, the company will not change the world or create revolutionary products.

The Entrepreneur

The entrepreneur is always smelling around for revenue and growth opportunities. When they look at the world, they see an opportunity to expand. They often like to take existing ideas, bring them to market, and scale them up. If the company isn't growing, they aren't happy. Without the entrepreneur the company will fail to make money on the artist's vision.

The Operator

The operator loves to organize chaos. They love to organize chaos because they do not like chaos. They want to break down the workflow into predictable systems and processes that can be duplicated so everybody knows what is expected of them, finishes their work, and is rightly compensated. Without an operator helping to run the machine, people get exhausted with the artist and entrepreneur and look for work elsewhere.

The person you are looking for who can install the *Management and Productivity Made Simple Playbook* will be an operator. If you hand this assignment to an artist, they will forget to show up at 75 percent of the meetings, and, when they do show up, they will likely pontificate wildly about how great the future will be, all the while listening to a Beatles album—probably backward, while asking their direct report whether they can "hear it."

When Doug came on staff, I didn't just ask if he could help us design a simple management and productivity playbook. I also asked him to install the playbook while training a direct report to manage that playbook once it was in full use. The person Doug trained is named Kyle Willis. After Doug left us to turn around another massive company, Kyle took over and has managed the system of meetings flawlessly. I can honestly say the *Management and Productivity Made Simple Playbook*, under Kyle's leadership, has helped our business enter into its most productive season and, not only that, has given me the best relationship I've ever had with the business.

Before installing the playbook, I felt like my business was a machine I was trapped inside of. Today, my business is a community of thoughtful people working diligently to serve clients. It gives me energy to play the part of CEO, artist, and visionary inside this community.

Once you've identified your operator, they will use the following step-by-step guide to install it.

The *Management and Productivity Made Simple Playbook:* A Step-By-Step Plan

Step One: Assign an operator to install the playbook.

1. If you are not going to run the playbook yourself, make sure the person who does is a true operator. They should love managing an existing playbook. They should be good with people but should also be truth tellers. Because so much of the playbook is about assessing performance, a team member who is too much of a people pleaser will frustrate the system. You are looking for a process-driven team member who is also an encouraging truth teller.

2. Your operator could have the title of COO, President, or Vice President. They could even be a high-level executive assistant if your business is too small for an

executive team. You don't need to overthink this.
There's no reason to get bogged down in titles.

3. Know that the person who handles the *Management
   and Productivity Made Simple Playbook* will be
   running your company. While you don't need to think
   about titles (beware of title inflation), once you put
   this person in that seat, and if they work out well,
   you've likely found your go-to person who can set you
   free as an artist or entrepreneur. Your attendance at
   the Leadership Meeting will be your touchpoint with
   the company. You will no longer feel like you are
   trapped inside the machine.

Step Two: Launch the weekly All-Staff Meeting.

1. Don't worry about installing the entire playbook at
   once. For the first few months, all you need to do is
   hold the weekly All-Staff Meeting. The weekly staff
   meeting will remind everybody on your team of the
   mission and, specifically, the three economic
   priorities.

2. If you do not know your three economic priorities, go
   back to Step One in the airplane framework: Business
   on a Mission. The main reason to have a weekly staff
   meeting is to review the economic priorities of the
   business and talk about how the entire team can move
   them forward.

3. If you do not have a team but work with contractors,
   ask if they would be willing to attend the All-Staff
   Meeting. You can call the meeting whatever you want;
   if contract workers are critical to your success, ask

them to attend. Depending on the state you live in (American audience) you may not be able to make attendance mandatory, but most contractors will want to attend the weekly meeting anyway because it will help them serve you with more efficiency.

4. Once your staff meetings start feeling good and the business is aligned around the three economic priorities, move on to step three.

Step Three: Add a weekly Leadership Meeting.

1. A weekly Leadership Meeting can take place directly after the All-Staff Meeting. This meeting is the least formal of all the meetings but it still has a template that will make sure it's effective and doesn't waste anybody's time.

2. If your business is small, your Leadership Meeting and your All-Staff Meeting may be combined. However, the agenda for both meetings should be different. Even though you will be holding the meetings back-to-back with the exact same people in attendance, do fill out both meeting templates.

3. If your business has a leadership team that is not the same as the overall staff, the weekly Leadership Meeting will help your leaders talk about what each of their departments is working on and invite other leaders to help remove roadblocks.

4. The weekly Leadership Meeting is designed to increase morale and a sense of community among the leaders of the team. Do not be surprised if some of

your leaders feel isolated in their jobs. This meeting
will help maintain team unity from the top down.

5. Consider a quarterly breakfast or lunch for your
   leadership team. Even though you meet every week,
   one meeting a month or one meeting a quarter could
   be set aside as special. There's nothing like sitting
   around a table and sharing a meal to create
   community.

6. Once your leadership team feels like a good, healthy
   community, consider launching Department
   Stand-ups.

Step Four: Add Department Stand-ups.

1. If your business is small, your All-Staff Meeting may
   suffice in channeling your focus around the three
   economic priorities. However, as you grow, you'll find
   your team members begin dividing into departments.
   Sales, marketing, design, development, production,
   and customer service are all examples of departments
   inside of a small, growing business. If you do have
   departments, go ahead and launch Department
   Stand-ups. These meetings happen every weekday and
   are intentionally brief. They're called Stand-ups
   because they are not supposed to be so long that
   people want to sit down. These meetings can take
   place in person or over conference calls.

2. The Department Stand-up is led by your department
   directors. If you own the business or are running the
   business, you should not need to attend these

Stand-ups. The template used to run the meeting will ensure the economic priorities still govern the mission.

3. Use the Department Stand-up template for every Stand-up meeting. Using the template is critical to the success of the *Management and Productivity Made Simple Playbook*. If you do not use the template, the conversation during the Stand-up will wander in unproductive directions.

4. Once your Department Stand-ups are up and running and going well, you can add step five of the *Management and Productivity Made Simple Playbook*.

Step Five: Add Personal Priority Speed Checks.

1. As your small business grows, individuals will find themselves more removed from the owner or the person running the business. This means they are going to grow a bit insecure about their performance. This can be a problem. If team members are not sure what their job is and/or whether or not they are performing well, individual and team morale begins to decline. If morale declines, productivity declines with it, resulting in the body of your airplane becoming larger and heavier. Each team member needs feedback in order to do their job well and to feel good about the role they play in the business.

2. One way to make sure team members are getting the feedback they need is to install a weekly Personal Priority Speed Check for every team member in the organization. The Personal Priority Speed Check Template should be filled out by the team member

before the meeting and then reviewed by their
department director during this check-in.

3. The Personal Priority Speed Check should be led by
   each team member's department head. The spirit of
   the meeting should be coach-like and encouraging.
   You will find that morale and productivity increase
   when you install the Personal Priority Speed Checks.
   Once your Personal Priority Speed Checks are up and
   running, you can implement step six of the playbook.

Step Six: Add *Quarterly Performance Reviews.*

1. Quarterly Performance Reviews are terrific for any
   size business. Even though this is step six in the
   process for a business with a dozen or more team
   members, a smaller business may want to implement
   this step sooner. Your people need to know how they
   are doing in the eyes of their department leader in
   order to feel comfortable and safe at work.

2. Use the Quarterly Performance Review Template to
   guide this meeting. The template should be filled out
   by both the team member and department head. Each
   template asks the person filling it out to assess the
   team member's performance. This sets up an open
   conversation about how the department head and
   team member see their performance. There may be
   areas where the team member feels they are doing a
   better job than the department head or, there may be
   areas in which they team member is insecure about
   their performance while the department leader feels
   they have done a good job. Either way, every team

member craves and deserves honest and encouraging feedback and the Quarterly Performance Review is where they are going to get what they want.

3. Once your small business has more than ten team members, you will likely want to start thinking about performance reviews that are tied to compensation packages. As a team grows, team members will want more predictability and control over their compensation. You can likely "wing it" when it comes to compensation packages for a while, but be careful. Offering discretionary bonuses and discretionary pay raises can get you into trouble. Every raise and bonus sets a precedent and, with it, an expectation. Holding Fourth-Quarter Performance Reviews tied to compensation creates a consistent, stable environment for a team member to thrive within.

4. The first three Quarterly Performance Reviews will help your team member understand what they should continue to do and what changes they might make to enjoy their full opportunity in terms of a raise and bonus. It's important to know this is the controlling idea behind the entire conversation: What do I need to do to get my full bonus and full pay raise next year?

5. When a team member feels in control of their financial future, they are more likely to love their job.

6. Here is a simple breakdown of raises and bonuses that could be made available to each team member: A 1 percent to 3 percent raise can be given to each team

member based on their performance. In addition, a 1 percent to 3 percent (of their salary) bonus can be tied to the overall revenue goals of the company. If the company hits its goal, up to 3 percent of their salary can be awarded to each team member, based on performance. If the overall business hits its stretch goal, up to 5 percent is made available to each team member. Every member on a perfect team on a perfect year would get a 5 percent bonus (of their salary) and a 5 percent raise. That may sound like a lot of money, but if you're hitting your stretch goals as a business, you've got a high-functioning team deserving of financial acknowledgment.

7. In order to run this playbook, your business will need revenue goals and stretch revenue goals. For instance, if your company makes one million dollars, team members have the opportunity to get up to 3 percent of their salary as a bonus. If the business hits their stretch goal of 1.3 million dollars, each team member could get up to 5 percent of their salary as a bonus. You can set the goals and stretch goals as you wish, and, naturally, the percentage each team member gets depends on their Quarterly Performance Reviews.

8. The Quarterly Performance Review and compensation system is a simple, scalable way to handle compensation. It may not be necessary for most small businesses but as you grow, you'll find the challenge of compensation and performance coming

up more often. This simple system should satisfy all of your team members because it allows them to control their financial future, sets clear expectations, and is designed to be fair.

Your Management and Productivity Meetings Are Not the Only Meetings You Will Have

The five meetings included in the *Management and Productivity Made Simple Playbook* are not the only meetings you will have; they are merely the set meetings you will have within a weekly and annual routine. These meetings are designed to replace most other meetings; however, you may also need to hold a few more meetings. Some of those meetings may include but are not limited to:

Revenue Meetings

The controller, operator, or some other financial leader in your small business should hold a monthly revenue meeting in which they review last month's numbers. After reviewing the numbers, two questions need to be addressed: Why and where did we do well? Why and where can we improve? You will find that this meeting gives you great insight into the overall health of the business and directly affects your strategy. If it's possible, your operator should collect the data and lead the revenue meetings.

War Rooms

When a specific problem needs to be tackled, it's often effective to gather the principal team members in a room for a few hours to formulate a strategy in a War Room. If you are relocating or selling off inventory or launching a new product, War Rooms may be necessary. War Rooms should be led by the leader who felt the meeting was necessary.

Leadership Off-Site Meetings

There are times when it makes sense for your leadership team to spend an entire day together to talk about the state of the overall business. These meetings will be led by whoever sits in the operator position and are mostly designed to help them understand how best to move the company forward. The agenda for the meeting will change depending on the context, but the basic idea behind a Leadership Off-Site Meeting is for the operator to align the team around particular challenges and opportunities. In essence, this meeting is a catch-all for all the needs the business is currently processing. Leadership Off-Site Meetings can last all day and happen when needed.

The Body of Your Airplane Will Become Leaner When You Install the *Management and Productivity Made Simple Playbook*

Again, the main culprit of overhead bloat comes from the cost of labor. When it comes to cutting labor costs, you have two choices: You can either lay off some of your team, or you can transform your existing team into a lean, revenue-generating force. If it's possible, we highly recommend saving jobs and transforming each member of your team into revenue generators.

Of course, there are times when people need to be let go, but we hope these instances are rare and more related to fluctuations in the market than to the productivity of your team.

If you are hiring somebody to run your small business, their job description could be as simple as this: Install Step One and Step Five of the Small Business Flight Plan into our small business. If they do this well, and also hold a monthly revenue meeting, you have the equivalent of a terrific COO helping you grow your small business.

To install the *Management and Productivity Made Simple Playbook*, take the steps outlined in this chapter and use the meeting templates included in your Small Business Flight Plan.

Copies of the meeting templates are on the following pages. When you use the digital version at SmallBusinessFlightPlan.com, you and your team can archive all past meeting templates.

All-Staff Meeting   DATE

COMPANY PRIORITIES
BY _____

①

②

③

DEPARTMENT UPDATES

① _____

What has our department done or what are we going to do to move us towards our company goals?

How did we add value to our customers last week?

How are we adding value for our customers this week?

② _____

What has our department done or what are we going to do to move us towards our company goals?

How did we add value to our customers last week?

How are we adding value for our customers this week?

③ _____

What has our department done or what are we going to do to move us towards our company goals?

How did we add value to our customers last week?

How are we adding value for our customers this week?

Access a digital, fillable version at SmallBusinessFlightPlan.com

Leadership Meeting   LEADER FOR THIS MEETING

(1) _____

What big initiatives are happening this week?

Is there anything blocking these initiatives?

Who is responsible for completing each task?

(2) _____

What big initiatives are happening this week?

Is there anything blocking these initiatives?

Who is responsible for completing each task?

(3) _____

What big initiatives are happening this week?

Is there anything blocking these initiatives?

Who is responsible for completing each task?

Access a digital, fillable version at SmallBusinessFlightPlan.com

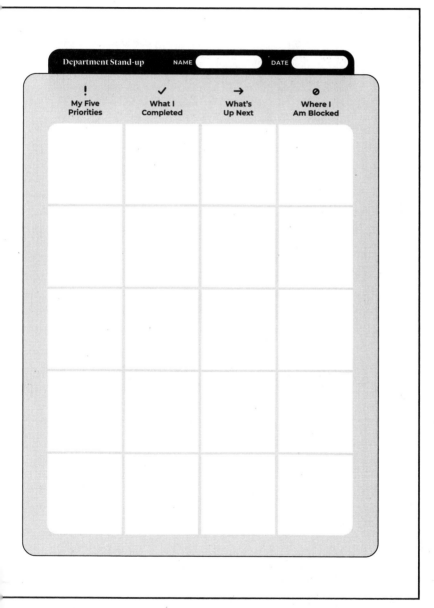

Access a digital, fillable version at SmallBusinessFlightPlan.com

Personal Priority Speed Check   NAME

COMPANY PRIORITIES
BY _____

① _____   ② _____   ③ _____

MY DEPARTMENT'S TOP PRIORITIES
Time-bound · Measurable · Specific

1. _____
2. _____
3. _____
4. _____
5. _____

MY PERSONAL PRIORITIES
Timebound · Measurable · Specific

1. _____
2. _____
3. _____
4. _____
5. _____

MY DEVELOPMENT PRIORITIES

1. _____
2. _____
3. _____

Access a digital, fillable version at SmallBusinessFlightPlan.com

Quarterly Performance Review

NAME

PERSONAL PRIORITIES	EXCEEDED	MET	DIDN'T MEET
#1: Comments	☐	☐	☐
#2: Comments	☐	☐	☐
#3: Comments	☐	☐	☐
#4: Comments	☐	☐	☐
#5: Comments	☐	☐	☐

Came prepared to Personal Priority Speed Checks?	☐	☐

NEXT OPPORTUNITIES

Once you have taken the first five steps, you'll find your small business is making a lot more money. So how do you manage that money? Let's move on to the last of the six steps: Small Business Cash Flow Made Simple.

6

Cash Flow

STEP SIX:
Fuel Tanks

*Get Control of Your Finances With
Small Business Cash Flow Made Simple*

Step Six Will Help You Solve These Problems:

- You aren't sure where your personal finances and the business finances begin and end.
- You consistently worry you are going to run out of cash.
- You get profit-and-loss statements from your accountant but they seem confusing and don't help you make decisions.
- You aren't sure how much profit the company really makes.
- You want the small business to help you make outside investments that build personal wealth.

- You want extra money to reinvest back into the business for hiring, new technology, advertising, and more.
- You need real-time optics into how your small business is doing financially.

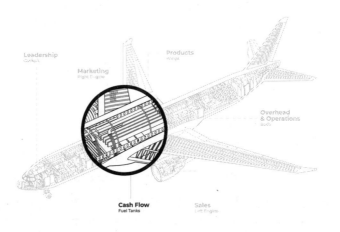

. . .

If you manage the six parts of your business well, it should grow, and you'll start making more money. This brings us to the final step in our list: Small Business Cash Flow. Even if your business is engineered like the perfect airplane, it is shockingly easy to run out of money and crash your plane.

As it concerns our airplane metaphor, the way you manage the money coming in and out of your business is represented by the fuel tanks. If you have plenty of fuel, you can fly your airplane far and fast. More than that, you can circle the airport when there is trouble and secure yourselves plenty of time to fix whatever is wrong.

Stories have been told about pilots who have circled airports addressing a problem with their plane only to crash because they ran out of fuel. No matter how big and beautiful your airplane is, without fuel, it's going down.

So, how do we manage money in such a way that we can pay our bills, enjoy a great salary, put some profit away for a rainy day, pay our taxes, leverage our success into a diversity of outside investments, and, most importantly, never run out of money?

The answer: Manage your small business cash flow using five checking accounts.

You Don't Have to Sweat the Finances

I created the *Small Business Cash Flow Made Simple Playbook* by accident. Like many small-business owners, when I started my business, I operated with only two accounts: my personal account and my savings account. My business expenses, along with my personal expenses, all came out of my personal account. This was a huge mistake not only because it made filing taxes difficult, but it blurred the line between my business and my personal life. At the time, I had no employees and really didn't see a difference between what I spent to make money and what I spent to eat and live. Because my company was being run out of my personal checking account, though, I found it hard to know where the company was succeeding and where I was bleeding it dry.

Slowly, I began to add more accounts to my banking system. I added an operating expense account, so I could keep track of the money going in and out of the company. A couple of years later, after I got tired of not having enough money for taxes, I opened an account to set aside tax money in advance. From there I added an account for a rainy-day fund, and so on. I'll explain each account and how I use them a little later.

Soon, I realized I'd created a terrific money-management system for a guy who hates managing money. I love to make money, but I'm not the type to sit and count every dollar and review the budget and pore over profit-and-loss statements for hours.

The *Small Business Cash Flow Made Simple Playbook* is perfect for business owners and leaders who identify more as moneymakers than as money managers. That's not an excuse; we all need to steward our money well. It's just that most entrepreneurs like making it more than managing it.

Here is what running my money with five checking accounts has allowed me to do:

- I can log onto my online banking portal and see the overall health of my company in an instant.
- When I log onto my banking portal, I know how much money my wife and I have and how much money my business has. I know that I only have access to one of those piles of money. I never dip into the company for personal gain.
- I am never short of cash when the tax man comes. I can pay taxes, and it never bothers me (okay, maybe a little) because I've already psychologically separated myself from the money I will pay the government.
- I know the business can suffer a loss and/or survive a crisis and we will not have to lay anybody off because I have plenty of money put away for a rainy day.

- When I log onto my online banking portal, I can see how much money my wife and I are putting away to create personal wealth for ourselves and our family. My business exists to generate money I can use to buy financial products and investments that will make my family even more money generations into the future.

If all of this sounds too good to be true—especially for somebody who likes making money more than managing money—you're going to enjoy the *Small Business Cash Flow Made Simple Playbook*. You no longer have to sweat the finances.

The *Small Business Cash Flow Made Simple Playbook*

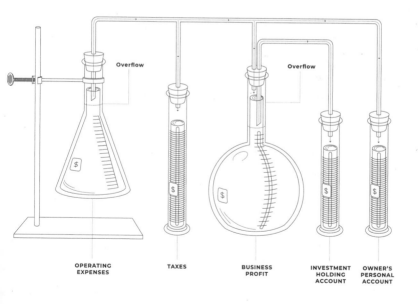

OPERATING EXPENSES TAXES BUSINESS PROFIT INVESTMENT HOLDING ACCOUNT OWNER'S PERSONAL ACCOUNT

The five checking accounts you will use to manage your small-business finances flow in and out of each other to create a fluid system that will give you optics, and control, over your money.

Here is a detailed description of each of the five checking accounts and a breakdown of how to use them.

Operating Account

All of the money that flows into and out of your business will flow into and out of this account. This is the main account you will use to pay all your bills, including your personal salary. Yes, you have to establish a personal salary. It's critical to the health of your business.

Personal Account

Your Personal Account will receive an automated bimonthly or monthly transfer from the business account that will make up your personal salary. How much money you pay yourself depends, and it's largely up to you. If your new business is a side hustle, you might pay yourself very little so you can get the machine going. If your business is established, you can and should pay yourself much more. You deserve it. You will figure out how much you can pay yourself as you go along. The key principle, though, is this: You must live off of a fixed salary so the business can establish a predictable rhythm, allowing you to manage and grow the business. As the business grows, you can give yourself raises. Don't forget: Your salary, unlike everybody else's salary, is taxable income. I'll show you how to put tax money aside in a minute.

Business Profit

Your Business Profit Account is where you store the money your business makes that does not need to go back into the company in order to keep it alive. You will establish a high-water mark for your Operating Account. When you have excess money in the Operating Account, you will transfer money into your Business Profit Account. The high-water mark will be different for everybody and will change as your business grows. This account will also serve as your rainy-day fund you can dip into if the business suddenly encounters a headwind and starts burning more fuel.

Tax Account

Your Tax Account is where you will put the money you'll use to pay or pre-pay taxes. This account will serve you in two ways: First, it will give you peace of mind that you will always be able to pay your taxes (while stopping you from spending the money elsewhere) and second, it will act, in some ways, as a secondary safety account. I'll explain a little more about that later.

Investment Holding

Your Business Profit Account is the place where you put money and keep it for a rainy day, but if that account grows so large that it doesn't make sense to keep all of it as an emergency fund, you'll move that money into an Investment Holding Account and decide from there what to do with it. As the name suggests, I recommend using this money to buy outside investments that will make you even more money without you having to work for it. You can invest in real estate, stocks, insurance products, CDs, cryptocurrency, whatever you want. If you want to buy a second home or a bass boat or a family vacation in Europe, you can do that from this account too. Your Investment Holding Account holds the money the company made for you. It's your money. Still, if you invest your money rather than spend it, your money will start making even more money and that's the money the uber-wealthy like to live off of. Making money off of money is how many of the ultra-wealthy get and stay wealthy. In other words, your business is a machine that makes you money so you can buy another machine that makes you money. The difference between the first and second machine is that you have to work in the first machine and the second machine makes money without you working at all.

Should You Take Out Your Profit First?

If you're familiar with Mike Michalowicz and his book *Profit First*, you'll see a resemblance between my playbook and his. I promise, I didn't steal Mike's ideas. On a long drive one summer I listened to Mike's book and realized, for the first time in my life, I was not a complete idiot when it came to managing the company money.

For years I'd used this playbook and had never run into financial trouble, but I always wondered if it was just a band aid. I thought real businesspeople likely do it differently or had a better system, but Mike's book taught me that I was getting a lot more right than I was getting wrong.

Since I listened to his book, Mike and I have become friends. In fact, I will never write a book about my small-business cash flow system because Mike has already written it. If you want to take a deep dive into how to run your business using five checking accounts, read or listen to *Profit First*.

That said, there are two things I do differently than Mike. The main point of Mike's book is that you should take a fixed percentage of revenue out of the company at the beginning of each month. The money you take out first is the profit you are projected to make that month. This forces you to reverse engineer a business that makes you a profit. I, on the other hand, take profit out of the company sporadically based on whether or not the Operating Account has a surplus of cash. In other words, I take the profit that "boils over" a high-water mark in my Operating Expense Account. If I took our projected profit out at the beginning of the month like Mike, I'd likely take less, not more money, out of the company for profit. My business often closes very large deals every other month or so, which means revenue spikes sporadically. When that happens, I scoop the profit out of and away from the business. If I took the profit out first, based on a fixed percentage, I'd constantly have to transfer money back into the company to keep it afloat or, in reverse, have way too much money in my Operating Expense Account and be too tempted to spend it.

Mike also recommends that the account I call Investment Holding should be opened at a separate bank that does not show up in your online banking portal. He truly wants that money out of sight. This is smart, but I prefer having all my accounts visible in one online banking portal.

Am I wrong to pull the profit out sporadically? Is Mike right to pull his out as a fixed percentage at the beginning of the month and place it in a blind account? I think both systems are a considerable improvement on the ways that many of us are managing our money.

Now that we understand the basic philosophy of the playbook, let's break down the process of installing the playbook.

How to Install the *Small Business Cash Flow Made Simple Playbook*

Step One

Go to your bank and open five checking accounts. Those accounts should be your Operating Account, your Personal Checking Account, your Tax Account, your Business Profit Account, and your Investment Holding Account. You may already have some accounts like this; if you do, you'll want to rename them to reflect their appropriate functions. In addition, make sure they all show up in your online banking portal so you can see the amounts in each account comparatively and at a glance. This is the key to having a clear picture of where your business stands financially.

Step Two

Make sure all the money for your business flows in and out of your Operating Account. All revenue from the business should flow into this account, and all bills should be paid out of this account (except for taxes, which are paid out of the Tax Account).

Step Three

Your bimonthly or monthly salary should flow out of your Operating Account, and that salary should be fixed, just like all your employees'. You should not take more money out of the Operating Account if you want to buy a car, an expensive watch, or an albino tiger. The key here is to decide how much you want to make and live off of that amount for a long time. The benefit of paying yourself a salary is mostly for mental clarity. This way you know what money belongs to you versus what money belongs to the machine that exists to make you more money.

Step Four

Establish a high-water mark for your Operating Account. By this I mean an amount of money high enough to cover the largest hit you might experience that month. For instance, if your payroll is $25K every two weeks, you never want your account to go below $35K or so. If you get hit by payroll, you'd be down to $10K, but you'd have two weeks to make it up before you get hit again. Let's say your high-water mark, then, is $35K. That's pretty good; this amount keeps you safe yet doesn't allow a ton of excess money to sit around in your Operating Account (where people tend to spend it, and fast). Let's say you look at your account one day and you had $60K in cold, hard cash. That means you've got $25K over your high-water mark sitting there doing nothing. What you're going to do is take the excess $25K and split it between your Business Profit Account and your Tax Account. Simply log on to your online banking portal and transfer $12.5K to your Business Profit Account and $12.5K to your Tax Account. What results is your Operating Account is at $35K while your Business Profit Account increases by $12.5K and you've also put away $12.5K for taxes.

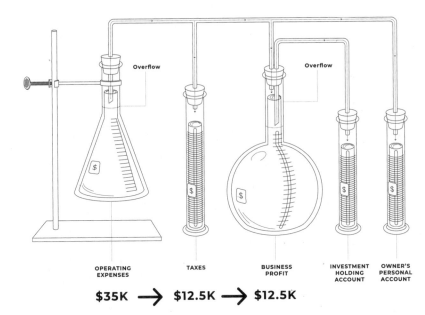

OPERATING EXPENSES   TAXES   BUSINESS PROFIT   INVESTMENT HOLDING ACCOUNT   OWNER'S PERSONAL ACCOUNT

$35K → **$12.5K** → **$12.5K**

What's great about this playbook is you can easily look at your Business Profit Account and know how much money is yours (on top of your salary) and feel good about how your business is doing. You can also look at your Tax Account and feel great about the fact that you have plenty of money to pay your quarterly business and salary taxes. In fact, you'll probably be transferring into your Tax Account so that, at the end of the year, you'll have an excess of money in your Tax Account that can be moved into your Business Profit Account. That dynamic is the exact opposite of what most small-business owners experience come Tax Day, so that day will feel great for you.

Step Five

Just like your Operating Account, you will also establish a high-water mark for your Business Profit Account. You will want to work up to and keep your Business Profit Account at or above that high-water mark because your Business Profit Account is also your rainy-day fund. I believe your Business Profit Account should be about six times your Operating Account's high-water mark. If your Operating Account's high-water mark is $35K, your Business Profit Account's high-water mark should be $210K. I realize that's a lot of money sitting there not earning much interest, but that money is going to buy you one of the most valuable things a small-business owner can have: peace of mind.

When you have six times your Operating Expense Account's high-water mark, you have a reserve fuel tank that will allow you six months' worth of circling the airport in the event of a crisis. With such a rainy-day fund, you can slowly adapt and even pivot in harsh weather or malfunctions in the plane. No more losing sleep over whether or not you will have to lay people off or crash-land the plane.

As your business grows, it will likely start to bother you to have so much money sitting in a basic checking account. If inflation starts to increase, that money really is being devalued by the day. If this becomes true for you, congratulations. You're sitting on a pile of cash. Feel free to take some of the money in your Business Profit Account and put it into a better investment that gets a higher interest or return rate, but the key is to make sure that money is liquid. There will be times each year when you've miscalculated and will need to move money back from your Business Profit Account to your Operating Expense Account. Hopefully those instances will be rare as you adjust high-water marks and get a sense for when to transfer money into profit and taxes, but everybody experiences cash flow fluctuations. Regardless, the Business Profit Account mitigates the pain of those disruptions.

Remember this as well: Whenever you move money backward from Business Profit, you can move the same amount backward from taxes because that money is no longer taxable income. In other words, if you suddenly need $10K, you can move $5K back from Business Profit and $5K back from Taxes.

So, what do you do when your Business Profit Account has a glut of cash? Let's say you check your account and transfer some money so that you have $250K in your Business Profit Account when your high-water mark was $210K. That means your business is now a true, profit-producing machine. This money is all yours. You can do with it what you want. However, before you buy the nautical brass collapsing telescope used in the filming of *Pirates of the Caribbean 4,* do take time to move that money into your Investment Holding Account. Why? Because the very name of that account is going to pressure you to invest that money rather than buy the telescope (even though there are only nineteen left). The money that ends up in Investment Holding is the money that can seriously contribute to your personal wealth.

Betsy and I used money from our Investment Holding Account to build our home with cash and fund our retirement accounts. We also purchased life insurance, put money in the stock market, bought rental property, and contribute to organizations we love. Betsy chairs the board of an anti-human trafficking organization and we use money out of Investment Holding to donate to the organization and host a large dinner every year in which we raise even more money. The great thing is we do all of this from a position of stability because the machine we built has allowed us to be strategically and predictably generous.

If you want to splurge using money from Investment Holding, feel free. But if you wait and buy your albino tiger from the money you make off your investments, you can have the tiger as well as future revenue that your investments continue to produce.

As I said at the beginning of this chapter, I am more wired to make money than manage it, yet I never feel the frustration of that fact. We always have the money to move the company forward, pay our taxes, live off of, and invest.

Should Your High-Water Marks Change as the Business Grows?

If you implement your Small Business Flight Plan, your business will grow. I remember years ago being kind of shocked scrolling through my Instagram feed when a friend publicly celebrated that their small business made two million dollars. I sat there and thought of that kind of success as impossible. But I kept running my business using the playbooks and frameworks you've just read about and within two years my company was bringing in more than three million dollars and continued to grow at double-digit percentages for years and years after and continues to grow today.

Don't be surprised if your small business grows a great deal bigger than you imagined. If this happens, though, the high-water marks in your Operating Expense and Business Profit Accounts should change as your business expenses increase. Your high-water mark may need to change from $35K to $55K depending on how much money your business is bringing in and spending. How do you know when your high-water marks need to change? You will know when the hits to your Operating Expense Account start to get so large, they bring your balance closer and closer to zero. When that starts happening, congrats! It just means all the numbers are getting bigger, including your Investment Holding balance!

Of course, it may be true that you have partners in your business or other complications, such as investors. Not to worry. The key is to split up the Investment Holding Account according to a cadence agreed upon by all parties. The playbook works fine even with outside investors.

The great thing about the *Small Business Cash Flow Made Simple Playbook* is that it will grow with your business. Whether you're managing a side hustle that makes $20K per year or have grown your business north of $100 million, the playbook works to help you make even more money and to preserve your sanity.

7

How to Install the Small Business Flight Plan

Okay, now that we know what we have to do to clarify our mission and Guiding Principles, ramp up our marketing, close more sales, optimize our product offering, streamline our productivity, and manage our cash flow, how do we actually implement the entire playbook?

In the final chapter we will look at the various ways you can implement the Small Business Flight Plan. Regardless of whether you are a B2B business, B2C, nonprofit, solo-preneur, start-up, growth company, or $100-million success story, the Small Business Flight Plan can work for you.

Growing a small business can be an exhilarating journey. It can also be a burden and, quite frankly, a financial disaster that causes misery for years to come. There are many factors that determine the difference, of course, but once you have a good product people actually want and are able to get it to market, much of the rest of the journey amounts to simple business building. I say simple because we make it far more complicated than it needs to be.

The six steps that will help you implement your Small Business Flight Plan will not solve every problem you have as a small-business leader, but they will solve most of them. In fact, the flight plan will preempt the causes of most small-business catastrophes.

Feel free to nuance the steps. I know plenty of small-business owners who added core values to their Guiding Principles or who hold their Leadership Meetings daily rather than weekly, for example. Certainly if you implement the frameworks and play-books as they are designed, you will have success, but you know your business much better than I do and you will know intuitively where you need to make custom adjustments. That said, if you encounter problems, ask yourself honestly if implementing the steps as they are presented might solve those problems.

Feel Free to Take It Slow

Feel free to take your time implementing your Small Business Flight Plan. If you try to do everything at once, you might get overwhelmed. But if you implement each step one after another and only move on when the previous step feels solidly embedded in your operations, you can transform your entire small business in under a year.

You do not have to implement the flight plan in the order we've listed the steps. In fact, if you're having cash flow issues, you might start with Step Six and open the five checking accounts that will give you better optics into how your money flows. After that, you might install Step Three so you can close a few big sales and get some money moving through those accounts. Then, when the business is stabilized, you can go back and install Step One and work on from there. If it helps, we've built an assessment at MyBusinessReport.com that will allow you to analyze the six parts of your business and issue a report detailing where your business needs the most work.

Three Ways to Implement the Small Business Flight Plan

There are three ways to implement the Small Business Flight Plan. The first is to use this book and do it yourself. You truly have everything you need in this book to get going. If you have the audio book, give it a listen as you commute or as you work out in the morning. If you've printed out your Small Business Flight Plan, look it over as you learn so the process itself will become more and more simple to execute.

If you learn better by watching video, each of the steps has a corresponding on-demand course at BusinessMadeSimple.com. The fee to subscribe to the platform is ridiculously low and it will walk you through the entire process. The platform also includes a digital Flight Plan allowing you to archive all past worksheets. You can run your small business from one online source.

You can also hire a coach to take you through the process. We've certified coaches all over the world to help small-business owners transform their small businesses. Many of our coaches host small groups so you may be able to implement your flight plan with friends. I actually attend a monthly small group myself because I've gotten so much value from other small-business owners who share best practices and encouragement. You can find a listing of our trained and certified Business Made Simple Coaches at HireACoach.com.

Growing a Small Business Can Be Fun and Rewarding

I've known more than a few small-business owners who, honestly, would be much better off working for somebody else. The anxiety that can be caused by the fluctuating tides of halt and progress can be mind numbing, not to mention the financial insecurity that often comes with the journey. My hope is that the Small Business Flight Plan does more than help you build your small business; my hope is it makes you a better mother or father, a better husband, a better wife, and a better friend. Nobody is made whole by financial security, but if they know how to handle success, they can be made more present. My wife and I don't fight about finances very often because we run the *Small Business Cash Flow Made Simple Playbook*. We don't fight about where the business is going because we have created our Guiding Principles. We don't worry about waste because we run the *Management and Productivity Made Simple Playbook*. I don't worry about cash flow shortages because I know I can close sales by inviting customers into a story. I don't worry about wasting money on marketing because our message has been made clear.

I love my small business. I love that I have an incredible team who come alive doing their jobs. I love that I get to play my part, creating content and perfecting our frameworks. I love that Betsy and I are starting to build a financial legacy our daughter will someday enjoy. Of course, we all dream about having a small business that sets us free. What I never expected, though, was to have so much fun getting here. Even though my business is doing well, I sort of miss the adventurous days trying to figure out everything in this book. I know it's a lot, but don't forget, it's fun. Standing around on the top of a mountain is great, but getting there is where all the memories happen.

As small-business leaders, you and I are America's leading employers. More people work for small businesses than the top ten American corporations combined. That means if you and I professionalize our operations, the teams that work with us have more security, better benefits, more clarity about why their work matters, and, if we're successful, more pay. I say all this to emphasize that the work you're doing to build your business is important. The quality of people's lives, including yours, improves as we do the work.

Here's to the success of your small business. If there is anything else I can do to help you, please let me know. Until then, have a safe flight.

Small business owners everywhere are accepting the challenge to double their small business revenue by creating their Flight Plans together in our community. We'd love to have you join the community at SmallBusinessFlightSchool.com.

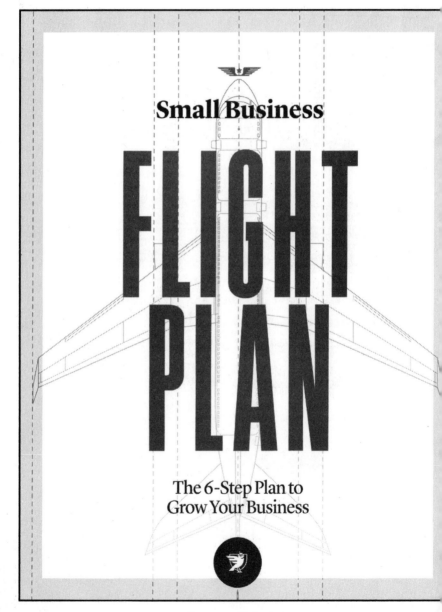

SmallBusinessFlightPlan.com

01

Leadership

The Cockpit

*Transform Yourself and Your Team
Into a Business on a Mission*

The most important thing a leader can do is provide a
unifying vision to the people they lead. The Business
on a Mission Framework is going to help you create
and communicate a vision that ensures the growth of
your small business.

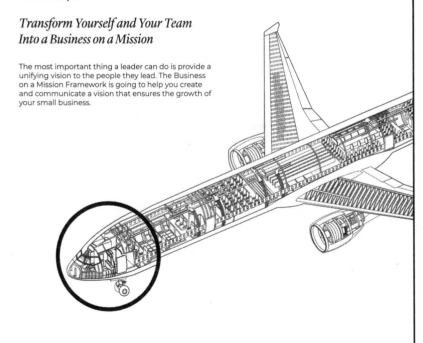

Business on a Mission
Guiding Principles Worksheet

MISSION STATEMENT

KEY CHARACTERISTICS

① ② ③

CRITICAL ACTIONS

① ② ③

02

Marketing
Right Engine

Clarify Your Message So Customers Will Engage

More than 700,000 small-business owners have clarified their message using the StoryBrand Messaging Framework. When you clarify your message, more customers will place orders.

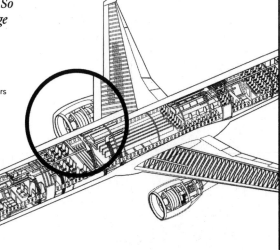

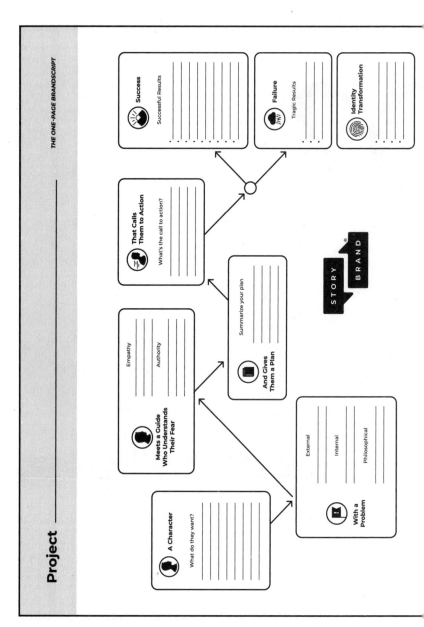

03

Sales

Left Engine

Stop Selling, Make the Customer the Hero, and Invite Them Into a Story

Very few people like to sell. But if you own or lead a small business, you have to. *The Customer Is the Hero Sales Framework* helps you stop selling and invites customers into a story. It's the sales framework for people who hate to sell. And it works.

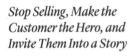

The Customer Is the Hero SalesScript

Business Made Simple

① Start with a problem

② Position your product as the solution

③ Give the customer a step-by-step plan

④ Paint the stakes (negative)

Paint the stakes (positive)

⑤ Call the customer to action

Use this formula to create sales copy fo
- Sales conversatio
- Sales letters
- Proposals
- Presentations

04

Products
Wings

*Optimize Your
Product Offering for
Revenue and Profit*

The best way to increase
your profit margin is to sell
more of the products that
generate the most profit. Few
business leaders really know
where their profit is coming
from. After you optimize your
product offering for profit, you
will know exactly how to make
more of it.

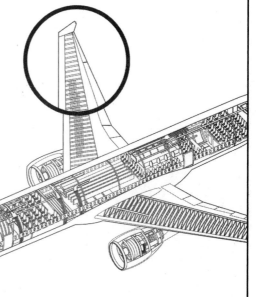

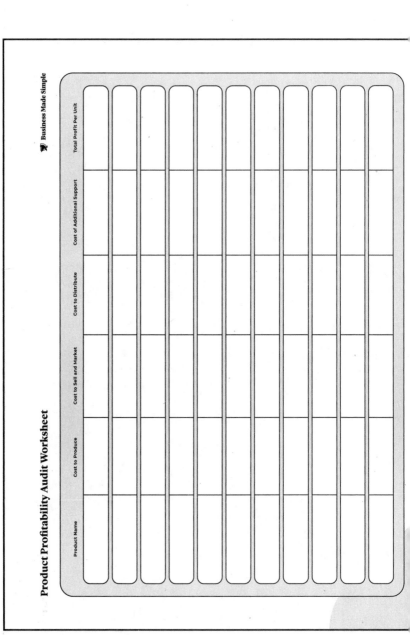

Product Profitability Audit Worksheet

👉 Business Made Simple

Product Name	Cost to Produce	Cost to Sell and Market	Cost to Distribute	Cost of Additional Support	Total Profit Per Unit

Product Brief Worksheet   🦅 **Business Made Simple**

Project Owner: _____

PRODUCT NAME

1. What is the product name? _____

2. Does it describe the product well and tease the value?

3. Will the name be confusing or create a problem in the marketplace?

PRODUCT DESCRIPTION

1. What problem does this product solve for our customer?

2. How does the product resolve the customer's problem?

3. Describe the benefits the customer will experience if they use the product:

4. Describe the features of this product and how it's going to help customers:

CORE MESSAGING

1. Who are we selling this to?

2. Do we have access to the target market for this product, and if so, how?

3. How will we define the customer's problem for marketing collateral?

4. What is our one-liner?

HIGH-LEVEL MARKETING RESEARCH

1. Is there a proven demand for this product in the marketplace?

2. Have we sent out a customer survey ensuring our customers would want this product? What questions did we ask in the survey and what were the results?

3. If we offer this product, who will we be competing with?

    a. Are we priced above or below the competition?

    b. How are we positioned against the competition? (What makes our product better?)

FINANCIALS

1. What is the price of this product and how did we determine this price?

2. Will it be profitable?

3. How much will this cost us to build? How much will this cost us to maintain? (Do we need to hire support staff, more tech support, etc?)

4. Who will be responsible for revenue related to this product?

SALES PROJECTIONS (BASED ON CURRENT CUSTOMER BASE)

1. What are the 30-60-90-day sales goals?

2. What's the first-year revenue projection related to this product?

3. What's the goal for units sold in the first year?

PRODUCT VALIDATION

1. Will this product cause any problems with existing products?

2. Will this product upset any existing or future customers? Why?

KEY DATES

1. When will this product be launched?

2. When will the landing page for this product be created?

3. When will the prerelease announcement be made to current customers?

SALES AND MARKETING PLAN

1. When will we check off the key sales and marketing components of this product?

    a. One-liner: _____
    b. Landing page: _____
    c. Lead generator: _____
    d. Nurture or sales emails: _____
    e. Social collateral: _____

05

Overhead & Operations
Body

Streamline Your Workflow
With Management and
Productivity Made Simple

The number one cost for most businesses is labor. But payroll shouldn't be a burden. When you align your team around three economic priorities and then get everybody working together to meet those objectives, your labor force remains lean because they are so productive. If you're having trouble creating a predictable, reliable workflow that builds your company rather than burdens it, the *Management and Productivity Made Simple Playbook* will work for you.

All-Staff Meeting   DATE

COMPANY PRIORITIES
BY _____

① ② ③

DEPARTMENT UPDATES

① _____

What has our department done or what are we going to do to move us towards our company goals?

How did we add value to our customers last week?

How are we adding value for our customers this week?

② _____

What has our department done or what are we going to do to move us towards our company goals?

How did we add value to our customers last week?

How are we adding value for our customers this week?

③ _____

What has our department done or what are we going to do to move us towards our company goals?

How did we add value to our customers last week?

How are we adding value for our customers this week?

Leadership Meeting　　　LEADER FOR THIS MEETING

(1) _____

What big initiatives are happening this week?

Is there anything blocking these initiatives?

Who is responsible for completing each task?

(2) _____

What big initiatives are happening this week?

Is there anything blocking these initiatives?

Who is responsible for completing each task?

(3) _____

What big initiatives are happening this week?

Is there anything blocking these initiatives?

Who is responsible for completing each task?

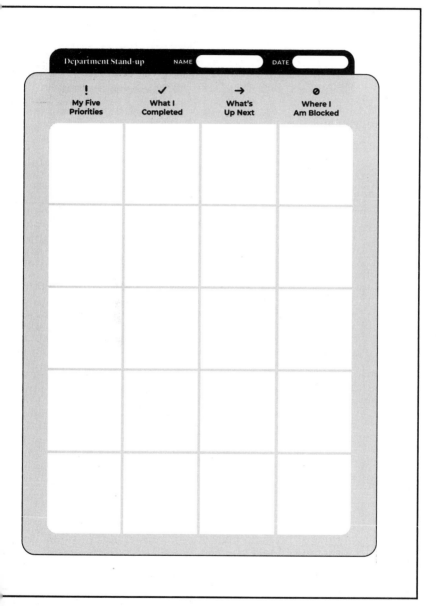

Personal Priority Speed Check   NAME

COMPANY PRIORITIES
BY _____

①

②

③

MY DEPARTMENT'S TOP PRIORITIES
Time-bound · Measurable · Specific

1. _____
2. _____
3. _____
4. _____
5. _____

MY PERSONAL PRIORITIES
Timebound · Measurable · Specific

1. _____
2. _____
3. _____
4. _____
5. _____

MY DEVELOPMENT PRIORITIES

1. _____
2. _____
3. _____

Quarterly Performance Review

NAME

PERSONAL PRIORITIES	EXCEEDED	MET	DIDN'T MEET
#1: Comments	☐	☐	☐
#2: Comments	☐	☐	☐
#3: Comments	☐	☐	☐
#4: Comments	☐	☐	☐
#5: Comments	☐	☐	☐

Came prepared to Personal Priority Speed Checks?	☐	☐

NEXT OPPORTUNITIES

06

Cash Flow

The Fuel Tanks

Manage Your Small Business Cash Flow Using These Five Checking Accounts

We've all read our profit-and-loss statements but do they really help you make decisions? Does your P and L help you understand how much money you have, how much money the business has, how much money you've set aside for taxes, how much profit the company is really making, and whether or not you have enough cash on hand to invest in a great investment opportunity? If not, manage your business with five checking accounts and you will have clarity (and security) moving forward. Small-business finance does not have to be complicated.

Business Made Simple's

Small Business Cash Flow Made Simple Playbook

Without cash, a business will crash. And while many small-business owners may know how to make money, they don't always know how to manage it. To ensure your business flies far and fast, install the *Small Business Cash Flow Made Simple Playbook*. When you do so, you will . . .

- Never accidentally run out of money. You will know well in advance whether your overall profit is shrinking.
- Always have the money to pay taxes, even surprise tax bills.
- Always have money for payroll.
- Know how much money YOU can actually take from the business.
- Have cash to invest back into the business which will set you up for growth.

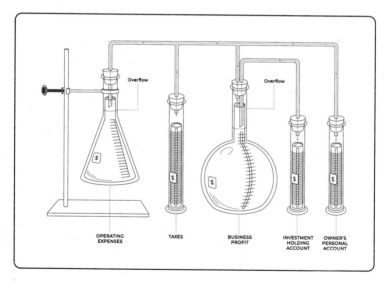

*Instructions for your Small Business Flight Plan can be found in the book *How to Grow Your Small Business* or through the online platform at **BusinessMadeSimple.com**.

SmallBusinessFlightPlan.com

Operating Account

This is the account that all money flows into and out from. All revenue will stream into this account and all bills, including the owner's salary, will flow from this account.

Personal Checking Account

This is the owner's personal account. The owner will take a fixed salary from the operating account once or twice a month and move it into the personal account. The owner does not take money from the operating account for personal use.

Business Profit Account

When the operating account goes over a certain predetermined amount, you scrape money off the top to put in your business savings account. Your business profit account will eventually grow to five or six times your monthly overhead. Your business profit account becomes the safety net for the organization.

Tax Account

Whenever you put money into your business savings account, you'll want to put the same amount of money in your tax account. Essentially, you will be splitting the excess money (true profit) your business is making between your savings and tax account. Putting 50% of your profit into your tax account ensures you will always have the money to pay taxes. In fact, because you are putting in 50% and tax rates are lower, you will be saving excess money for taxes and can give yourself a solid return at the end of the year.

Investment Holding Account

Your business profit account also has a pre-set top threshold that is five or six times your monthly overhead. When the business profit account exceeds that threshold, scrape the money off the top and put it into your investment holding account. This, then, is the money that is yours to do with whatever you like. We recommend taking that money and buying investments that make even more money and help diversify your revenue. For instance, you could use this money to fund your SEP IRA, buy property or other assets, or invest in the stock market.

Acknowledgments

Thanks to Bill Haslam for your incredible encouragement and kindness and for pointing out that I needed to professionalize my operation. And thanks to Doug Keim for helping me make it happen. I also want to thank my team, Kyle Willis, Kyle Reid, Dr. JJ Peterson, Matt Harris, Tyler Ginn, Jake Ousley, Marlee Joseph, Andy Harrison, Karri Ellen Johnson, Aaron Alfrey, Bobby Richards, Lindsay Frail, Sam Buchholz, Steven Parker, Kari Kurz, Amy Smith, Macy Robison, Hilary Smith, Kelley Kirker, Prentice Sims, Tyler Bridges, Rosie Hunt, Hannah Hitchcox, Suzanne Kelly, James Sweeting, Collin Smith, Zach Grusznski, Josh Landrum, Patrick Copeland, Suzanne Norman, Aundrea De Leon, Tim Schurrer, and Sydney Weidlich. A special thank you to Emily Pastina who manages all our projects and tells me every morning what I am supposed to be working on. She frees me up to be creative and I am grateful. Thanks as well to the hundreds of Business Made Simple Certified Coaches and StoryBrand Certified Guides who partner with us to help small-business owners grow their small businesses. Thanks also to our facilitators who are constantly on the road presenting workshops on our sales and marketing frameworks.

A special thanks to Carey Murdock who has kept me incredibly organized over the year it took for me to write this book.

I am also grateful for the long friendship and business relationships I've had with my agent and publisher. Wes Yoder is the world's best literary agent and has helped me dream up this book from day one. Sara Kendrick isn't just a great editor; she's a fun person and somehow delivers her criticism while still making me laugh. Jamie Lockard runs a steady ship us authors can count on, and Belinda Bass has been making great book covers for me for more than twenty years. I'd also love to thank Linda Alila for her editorial support and Andrew McFadyen-Ketchum for his copyediting.

I also want to thank my wife, who, morning after morning, gives me a kiss and sends me out the door to do work she also thinks is important because she cares about you, the small-business owner. We have so many friends in the fight and she wants to see them win. I love you, Betsy.

Lastly, thank you. Thanks for believing in yourself and your product and your people and your customers. I'll keep going as long as you keep going. I know it's hard, but I believe in you.

Index

About the Author

Donald Miller is the CEO of Business Made Simple and StoryBrand. He is the author of *Building a StoryBrand* and *Business Made Simple*, and is the coauthor of *Marketing Made Simple*. He is the host of the *Business Made Simple* podcast and can be followed on Instagram at @DonaldMiller. Donald lives in Nashville, Tennessee, with his wife, Betsy, and their daughter, Emmeline.

To accept the challenge of joining thousands of other small business owners in professionalizing their operations and doubling their revenue, visit SmallBusinessFlightSchool.com.